"*A World I Loved* is the work of a Lebanese woman whose life has been dominated by war. Wadad Makdisi Cortas was our *Passionaria*; a brilliant fighter, a rebel. But the arms she trusted were peaceful resistance, and education. Her narrative is seamless: the personal and the historical interaction in her book is one of the most meaningful and endearing covering of the Arab East in the 20th century, giving through personal testimony, soul and voice to millions of people sacrificed on the altar of world politics."

—ETEL ADNAN, author of *Sitt Marie Rose* and
In the Heart of the Heart of Another Country

"Wadad Makdisi Cortas elegantly interweaves fascinating personal narrative with subtle reflections upon the great political and social questions of her day: the transition from the Ottoman Empire to the mandate system; the rise of the nation state; the colonisation of Palestine and the struggle for its freedom; Nasserism; the tragedy of the Lebanese civil war; the fight for women's equality; the role of educators and the arts. Makdisi Cortas is the truest companion on this epic journey, inviting the reader to travel with her in the diverse worlds of Ottoman Syria, colonial Baghdad, mandate Jerusalem, depression-era America and 1960's Beirut. Out of fragments shattered by war and loss, she creates a crystal clear image of the world she loved and helped create, a world underpinned by artistic vision and triumphant humanity."

—KARMA NABULSI, Oxford academic and
former PLO representative

"This is far more than a memoir of a determined and independent-thinking Arab woman. It is a window into the many tragedies that affected the peoples of the Middle East in the course of the twentieth century. Yet, at the same time, reading the book transported me to happier times of carefree childhoods and lasting relationships that come from living in a world where everyone knows everyone else for a lifetime. Despite decades of political turmoil and social change, the spirit of people like Wadad Cortas is a testimony to the endurance of the human spirit."

—DR. LEILA FAWAZ, Issam M. Fares Professor of Lebanese and
Eastern Mediterranean Studies, Tufts University

A World I Loved

The Story of an Arab Woman

WADAD MAKDISI CORTAS

NATION
BOOKS

New York

Copyright © 2009 by Wadad Makdisi Cortas
Foreword © 2009 by Nadine Gordimer
Published by
Nation Books, A Member of the Perseus Books Group
116 East 16th Street, 8th Floor
New York, NY 10003

Nation Books is a co-publishing venture of
the Nation Institute and the Perseus Books Group.

Books published by Nation Books are available at special
discounts for bulk purchases in the United States by corporations,
institutions, and other organizations. For more information,
please contact the Special Markets Department at the Perseus Books
Group, 2300 Chestnut Street, Suite 200, Philadelphia, PA 19103,
or call (800) 810-4145, ext. 5000, or e-mail
special.markets@perseusbooks.com.

The footnotes for this book were prepared by JoAnn Wypijewski

Designed by Brent Wilcox

Library of Congress Cataloging-in-Publication Data
Qirtas, Wadad al-Maqdisi, d. 1979
    [Dunya ahbabtuha. English]
    A world I loved: the story of an Arab woman/ Wadad
Makdisi Cortas.
        p.   cm.
    Includes bibliographical references and index.
    ISBN 978-1-56858-429-4 (alk. paper)
    1. Qirtas, Wadad al-Maqdisi, d. 1979   2. Women—
Lebanon—Biography.   3. Lebanon—History—20th century.
4. Middle East—History—20th century.   I. Title.
    PJ7858.I73D813 2009
    305.48'892756920092—dc22
    [B]

                                                    2008043943

10 9 8 7 6 5 4 3 2 1

Contents

∾

This book is dedicated to all of my mother's former students, colleagues, relatives, and friends who knew and admired her.

Had it not been for JoAnn Wypijewski's meticulous editing, immense knowledge of the politics of the region, perception, and sensitive rendering, this book would not have seen the light of day. For this she has my eternal gratitude and admiration.

—MARIAM C. SAID

Foreword

∽

NADINE GORDIMER

There is a vast library of books about the Middle East, the majority, in the present, dominated by the Palestine-Israeli conflict. Here is a work like no other in that library. To begin with, Wadad Makdisi Cortas is neither a Muslim nor a Jew. She is a Christian, but as she sets down on her first page, hers is "the story of an Arab woman." And in her account of her life in Beirut there is no contradiction in this identity that represents a resolution between two opposing forces of human faith and power that have existed since before the Crusades.

Born in 1909 in Beirut, she is an original in all the best senses of the admiring term. Her account of her life up to the late 1970s is remembered with sharp intellect, vivid awareness of the political circumstances that form her judgments, critical and self-critical of the value she arrived at. There is no political rhetoric, although her perceptions of the machinations of the colonial powers, France and Britain, combining when it suited them in common purpose to retain possession of Arab lands after the First World War, are astute. There is no rhetoric in her calm and sometimes

delightfully wry perceptions of the difficulties she had to overcome as a female—although not a Muslim—in claiming independence of thought and activity, which feminists might wish
proudly to claim on her behalf. Her childhood in a well-educated,
worldly family gave her that sense of the place of humans not
above but in the world of nature, which brings her writing a feel
for landscape, the beauty of sea, sky, and earth as the support
needed to keep balance in the assault of disorder and violence
that has disrupted life in her part of the world.

She had opportunities to further her education and fulfill her
intention to become a teacher. In America she found among her
Indian and Arab students "how much we had in common"
against colonialism. Back in Beirut she became principal of the
national Ahliah School for Girls, where she was to spend her entire working life, if one can restrict such a woman for whom ac-
ceptance or personal responsibility toward agencies of justice and
fulfillment of life for others was more than a career. Palestine was
under British Mandate; Lebanon was under French Mandate.
"Like a stray bird returning to its home, I yearned to speak my
language, to read Arabic books, and to foster Arab independence
and solidarity," she writes. But under the academic program
forced on the school by the French ministry, instruction was in
French. Her bizarre professional situation was decreed under a
wider colonial one. Lebanon became independent of France only
in 1943, but even then France maintained an armed presence until
1946. The honesty of her reaction to a colonial educational edict
is strikingly admitted: "How much of a compromise should I
make to come to terms with my own people? That question preoccupied me as I could see that bit by bit Lebanon was being detached from its Arab roots." That compromise could not have
been easy; for her it did not lead to rejection of anyone, while as-
serting the rights of one's own people. This was clearly no grand

abstraction, it was in the practice of daily life. At her school there was a component of girls who were not Arab, neither Muslim nor Christian, even a few Jewish girls. None were discriminated against by headmistress, teachers, or other pupils; and at a distance of time this reads, rather than as an anachronism, as a microcosm of the future world Wadad Makdisi Cortas believed must be discovered, attained by human determination.

She emerges so unquestionably free of any racial or religious prejudice when she describes the attitude she shared with the people around her, family and friends in the Middle East, when "Ever since Hitler had come to power, throngs of people from several persecuted minorities had been fleeing to the Arab world." The reference is to Jews persecuted by Hitler: "From a human point of view we were worried about them and felt it our duty to offer them hospitality. But the numbers began exceeding expectations, and we felt driven into a difficult situation." This was an initial tolerance based on common human feeling that I think many, like myself, in a succeeding generation, aware of the horrific human crime of the Holocaust and the tragic strife between Arabs and Israelis to come, hardly know of. When the numbers of Jewish immigrants became many thousands, and finally the Balfour Declaration took part of Palestine itself as a national home of the Jews, this bond of common humanity she shows was inevitably, fatefully rent by Western-imposed frontiers that began and continued to be in fatal dispute. Her personal narrative of their disastrous effects ends with her last page in 1960, although they prevail today in many tragic forms, from the declarations of the Palestinian factions, Hamas and Jihad, that Israel has no right to exist, to the Occupied Territories created by the Israelis on Palestinian land and the vast wall built as the ultimate in brutal disruption of human concourse in the life of the Palestinians.

The world this remarkable woman loved and saw destroyed not only by "the Palestinian question" she anticipated as a student, but also by civil war within her own people, is strikingly created in her book, bringing one face-to-face with a unique personality and the contiguity of our living history.

November 2008

Introduction

∾

MARIAM C. SAID

According to her older sisters, my mother, Wadad Makdisi Cortas, exhibited a strong religious bent as a child. She prayed and read the Bible constantly. This alarmed her father; fearing that she would turn into a religious missionary, he decided not to send her to the American evangelical school her sisters attended, but to a secular, national one. The school he enrolled her in was the Madrasat Al Banat Al Ahliah in Beirut, established in 1916 by Marie Kassab. At the time, demand for girls' education was growing; the student body consisted of the many sects and religions that were in the region. My mother would spend most of her life there, first as a student, then briefly as a teacher, and for forty years, as its headmistress. From this platform, she would educate generations of young women. She had strong values, a civic consciousness, and a vision for the future of her country. These she never tired of articulating in public, which is clear from the story she herself tells in her book. In the end, her father had been quite perceptive; she did become a kind of missionary—but a secular one.

Her generation of women was not the first in what was then Greater Syria to be educated. Her mother and aunts had all earned a high school degree. (Her grandmother, her father's mother, had learned to read, as an adult, by taking Bible classes at a Protestant mission.) Some of these women, like Marie Kassab, and my mother's paternal aunt, Amina, who had been educated by missionaries, became teachers. Others, such as May Ziadeh and Julia Tohmeh Dimichkieh, became writers and advocates of women's emancipation. A few in my mother's generation achieved a higher level of education; they attended college and, in her case, graduate school.

From an early age, I became aware that my mother was different from the other mothers. She had a job; she was the headmistress of my school; and all the teachers and other students at school referred to me as 'bint el muddira' (the daughter of the headmistress). My aunts and my friends' mothers did not work. They were at home when their children came from school. It was my father's mother, Sitto Mariam, who was waiting for us when my three brothers and I came from school. She was in charge of running our house. All the other mothers were praised for their cooking and baking skills and for their knitting, sewing, and embroidery talents. My mother neither cooked nor knitted nor embroidered. She could not even sew on a button correctly. The other mothers wore colorful printed dresses and jewelry, had their hair done, and put on makeup. My mother wore dark suits with no makeup, and her hair was pulled back in a bun. The only jewelry she wore, on occasion, was a simple brooch or a thin string of pearls around her neck. This had not always been the case. According to my cousin Salwa, my mother, when she was young, was extremely coquettish and cared about clothes. Some of her early photographs attest to that. But by the time we were born, she had taken her role of headmistress very seriously and wore outfits suitable to her position in society.

Like most bourgeois families in Beirut, we lived quite comfortably, surrounded by loving relatives. Our three-story building was occupied not only by my parents, brothers, and me but also by my widowed grandmothers. Eventually, my maternal grandmother moved out to an adjacent building, and my mother's sister, Soumaya, and her family, moved into my grandmother's old apartment. Every few years, a reshuffling of living arrangements occurred among the extended family with the same result—all my aunts and uncles lived within two adjacent blocks in four buildings.

By the time my parents came home from work, at about seven o'clock, we would have been fed and bathed, and our homework was done. Our only contact with Mother was when she read a story to us before we were tucked into bed, around 7:30 P.M. Even the stories that she read to us were different from the ones the other mothers read. They were stories from the Bible, such as the tale of Lot, and Arab fables, in which the morals were clear. We had to beg her to read "Little Riding Hood" or "Hansel and Gretel." In winter, we would sit around the fireplace in the living room to listen to her. Before reading a story, Mother would start peeling oranges for us to munch on while she read. She would throw the peel into the fireplace, and as we ate the oranges and listened to her, we would be mesmerized by her voice and intoxicated by the orange smell being emitted from the fireplace.

During the weekends, my parents usually stayed at home. We children were in and out of our relatives' houses or played in front of our building with the neighborhood kids. My mother kept herself busy indoors—reading and writing—and moving through the rooms with a feather duster. She could not sit still.

My father was the opposite. He was a quiet man, who sat in the living room and loved to interact with his children. He and my grandmother spent hours with us, just talking, playing cards and board games.

We ate our meals with our parents on the weekends and had many lively conversations. The banter was lighthearted and anecdotal, but my mother never missed an opportunity to be instructive, even at table. She would point out the moral in our anecdotes, and would say, for example, this story reminds us not to waste time, or not to throw rubbish on the streets, or to respect our elders, or to help those in need, or to be nice to our neighbors.

Our home was open to all. Once, a group of Quakers came to visit Lebanon. They were on their way back from Salonika, where they were assessing an orphanage that was in financial trouble. Mother invited them to dinner. When Quakers visited, we said grace before dinner. (My father was also a Quaker.) Grace is a moment of silence for Quakers. Soup was served and we sat silently for a minute. My brothers, father, and I immediately noticed that the soup was scalded, which meant that we were not going to touch it. Invariably, when my mother heated up food, she put the fire on high and left it there. After grace was over, we sat quietly, not eating. When she noticed, she said to the guests, "My children do not want to eat the soup because it is burnt. And you have just come from an orphanage where children barely have food." The poor guests! They had no choice but to eat the soup.

In many ways, I think that my mother was like a nineteenth-century socialist, who carried the burdens of the world on her back. She believed that it was her job in life to continually struggle for justice, human rights, and equality for all people. When I was in first grade, Mother took me, and my brother Nadim to visit some friends. It was winter. It was drizzling, and the wind was very damp. A few blocks away from our house, near Bliss Street in Beirut, we saw two barefoot little boys our age, wearing tattered summer clothes, shivering, selling chewing gum. It was a sad sight, and mother was appalled. She said to us: "These children should not be on the street. They should be in school." Both of us had a shocked look on our faces, because we also felt compassion for them. Mother said we would go get them some warm clothes. We walked back home, and she got each of them a shirt, a pair of pants, a sweater, socks and shoes. We went into the entrance of a building, where she changed their clothes and told them to tell their parents to enroll them in public school. The kids were stunned. We bought some gum and left. The next day, while going to school by tram, we encountered the same boys. They had their old tattered clothes on. When she asked what had happened, they ran away. Then the superintendent from the building came out and explained that the man who drops them off to sell gum was furious. He had hit them and said, "No one will buy gum from you with these fancy clothes." She was upset that her spontaneous humanity did not make a difference, at least in this instance.

My mother rarely took no for an answer, however, and usually got her way. She always had a smile, and when she spoke, she sometimes appeared coy. She was pretty, five feet tall, and could be seductive without knowing it. No one could refuse her anything, partly because of her smile, her interest in people, and curiosity.

My father was a successful entrepreneur in the food-cannery industry and had built his business from scratch. He was six feet tall, handsome, a former athlete, and a tennis champion of Lebanon. He took care of buying the food and staples, all of the finances, and every important issue that arose. All of my friends loved him because he was friendly, tolerant, open, and warm. He accommodated my mother and rarely intervened or challenged her. This could be disappointing, because when I grew older and was at odds with my mother, I wanted him to take my side, but he never did. They worked in concert and rarely argued, at least not in front of us. He was no pushover though. He had his likes and dislikes, and what he wanted had to be done the way he decreed. He cared about the way food was prepared and presented at table, and he would never use a paper napkin. He loved clothes and was impeccably dressed at all times. My mother always waited for him to get ready before going out, instead of the other way around.

Unlike most men of his generation, my father was broadminded and liberal. He had accepted that my mother would continue working when they married. However, he insisted that she not draw a salary from her employment, because that would reflect badly on him. A man was supposed to support his wife. My mother consented because she did not care about money and was happy to use the funds for student scholarships.

In the 1950s, my father's business underwent a severe downturn. He had lost his largest client, the British army, and a substantial market, Palestine, in 1948; and when the breakup of the Syrian and Lebanese Customs Union took place, trade was restricted, and he had to close his factory in Syria, his largest market. I would see my father in the living room, worried, and engrossed in adding and subtracting figures on little pieces of paper or on the side of a newspaper, trying to solve his business problems.

To ease the situation, my parents decided to rent out our apartment in Beirut for the extra income and to move permanently to Brummana, my father's hometown in the mountains, overlooking Beirut and the Mediterranean Sea. We owned a lovely house there, with an arched veranda, and a ceiling made of visible pine trunks. Until then, my brothers and I had attended my mother's school, which accepted boys until the sixth grade;

they would now be enrolled in a Quaker school in Brummana, as day students rather than boarders, therefore saving a lot of tuition. Things were bad enough that my father agreed that my mother's salary should be reinstated. She also began to teach humanities at the Beirut College for Women to supplement the family income. (I believe that she really loved teaching, because she retained the job long after our financial situation improved.)

At the time, I was unaware of what was happening. Only when the furniture in our Beirut apartment was being moved out did I realize that a major event was occurring.

It was also decided, mainly by my mother, that I should continue my education at her school. For my mother, it was imperative that I, her only daughter, remain there and not attend the same school as my brothers near home. She felt she had to be an example to others. Thus I became a boarder at the school. To me, this was traumatic, even though the older students were very kind and sweet to the younger kids. I was ten years old. From early on, I felt sacrificed for a greater cause.

During my five years at boarding school, I saw my mother alone, every day for ten minutes, during mid-morning recess. I would go to her office to say hello, get a hug and a kiss, and a snack sent from home. The only other encounter with Mother was as the headmistress of the school, mostly during morning assembly, when she stood at the podium and delivered the daily thought. Occasionally, she would go up to the boarding area, open my closet, and tidy it up for me. This embarrassed me among my peers in school. The more she did this, the more I made a mess of my closet. The boarders were from all over the world. I desperately wanted to be one of them and accepted as such. So I developed a strategy that served me well: I was one of the students and had nothing to do with my mother. I rebelled when they did, disobeyed the rules, and behaved as they did.

On Wednesdays, the school session was half a day. We were allowed to leave the premises in the afternoon. My mother had little time for me on these afternoons. She was busy with her various committees and projects. I was entrusted to my aunt Salma, who lived and taught at the school, and who dragged me along with her wherever she was going.

During the weekends, I would go home to Brummana with my parents, but on Sundays, I would have to endure another of my mother's sermons at the Quaker meetings that took place at my brothers' school. These meetings were compulsory for the students, but other Quaker families also attended them. It was like going to church on Sunday. The Quakers would meditate for an hour, and if anyone felt moved to share his or her thoughts with the congregation, he or she would rise and do so. My mother never failed to stand up and express her thoughts there.

The summers in Brummana were more leisurely. My mother was at home but only rarely would she join my grandmother and aunts in the mornings on the terrace, where they sat chatting, knitting, embroidering, having coffee, and reading their fortunes in the coffee cups. She preferred to remain inside, reading and writing. It was Sitto Mariam and my aunts who taught me to knit, sew, crochet, and embroider. But my mother would emerge during her morning break to sit with us briefly, mostly as a listener. Then again, around noon, she would appear to remind everybody of the time. She would say to my grandmother, "It is already 12 P.M. We'd better start setting the table for lunch, and will lunch be ready at 12:30?" My calm, gentle grandmother would assure her that everything was under control, that lunch would be ready and on time, and that my grandmother had been doing this all her life. But my mother would nevertheless walk to the kitchen to make sure all was in order, and sometimes she would decide to interfere, and that would invariably disrupt the smoothness of the process. Her anxiety manifested itself in this manner from early in the morning until she went to bed.

As a child, I never realized how anxious she was. She seemed always focused on the next task at hand and was the only one in our family who was conscious of how important time was. But later I came to understand that some of her restlessness had to do with her not knowing what to do with herself if she was not occupied with projects.

She woke up early, headed straight to the bathroom, and was fully dressed and ready before 7 A.M. I rarely saw her in her nightwear. She always preached to the girls at school assembly about how important it was not to linger in their nightwear until noon. One must get up early, full of energy, even during vacation, dress immediately, and brace for the day. It was a refrain she never tired of repeating. At home she was outraged by the fact that, in spite of her preaching, we continued to sleep late in the morning, until ten or eleven o'clock during the holidays, and she devised many schemes to get us up. When we were little, there were tutors who appeared at 8 A.M., so that we would be up early and engaged intellectually, or there were tennis lessons. As teenagers, she knew she could not force us to get up early, nor could she devise a program of instruction, so she would walk briskly around the house, and we would hear her heels clicking as she moved back and forth; then she would open and shut drawers, closets, and doors noisily in the hope that we would be irritated by the sounds and get up. To her great chagrin, this never worked.

Another habit of hers was taking away our shoes, literally, from under our feet. Sitting in the living room, we tended to take off our shoes to stretch our legs on the coffee table. But the minute we stretched out, our shoes would disappear.

One summer, she decided to change all the hymns that were sung at school, because they were in English, and their content was religious. (Over the years, she lost her love for the Bible and deplored the role religion had played in the Middle East.) She spent her days reading Arabic poetry and choosing poems to adapt to the music. So every morning, beginning at about 8:30, she would practice a single bar or section for hours, like a student, plodding away. It drove us crazy. She was not only playing the piano, she was singing along to make sure the piece worked. By the end of the summer, her book of Arabic songs, based on hymnal music, was published.

Despite my mother's courage in so many areas, simple, ordinary tasks that others did automatically petrified her. She disliked going to a store and buying anything. She hated using money, in any shape or form. My father, or his driver, would drop her off and pick her up from school every day. If, for any reason, she needed to take a taxi, my Aunt Salma would order it, pay the driver, and tell him where my mother was going. Salma also chose the fabrics (the colors and material) for her clothes and arranged things with the dressmaker, who came to the premises. All my mother had to do was attend one fitting, during her lunch break. Money was something she was taught to dislike, a necessary evil. (I think this came from her mother.) When she finally did start to draw a salary, during her marriage, she would immediately hand the check to my father, and not once ask how it was going to be used.

Certain things made my mother uncomfortable or frightened her: drunkards and people who lost their tempers or acted irrationally. Unrestrained emotional behavior, in general, confounded her, and she wouldn't know what to do until she had regained her sense of safety. Once, she was flying from New York to Beirut. In those days, the trip across the Atlantic was fourteen hours. On the flight, across the aisle from her sat a relative of hers who was totally drunk. Mother was so scared of him that she covered her head with the blanket and turned the other way, avoiding eye contact for the entire trip.

What inhibited and frightened others, such as standing on a podium in front of a huge audience, she did without batting an eye. My aunt Mona liked to tell the following story about her: During World War II, the French governor general of Lebanon was going to participate in a large political rally, which my mother and aunt attended. A young Lebanese woman, whose French and Arabic was perfect, and who was known to be the best simultaneous interpreter at the time, was hired to do the job. The minute the governor entered the hall, the young interpreter had cold feet and fainted. A group of people tried to revive her and could not. No one knew what to do. The ceremony was about to begin. My mother said, "I will do it," and walked over to the podium and proceeded to translate simultaneously, as if she had been doing this all her life. Apparently, she managed quite well.

She never lost her temper and never ever hit us. She abhorred violence. When she disapproved of our behavior, she could convey it without uttering a word; her face expressed her displeasure, and we would immediately understand that we had done something wrong.

Praise for her children was rare. Whatever one achieved, she believed, most of the time it could be better, no matter how well one did it. It wasn't said quite that way, but it certainly was expressed to mean that. This was quite upsetting because I never felt confident about anything.

Throughout my teenage years, I kept my distance from my mother. When I was fifteen, I insisted that I be allowed to live with Aunt Soumaya, who had an extra room in her apartment, instead of at the school. And I had a simple rule: Whatever my mother was, I wasn't going to be. I loved fashion and low-cut American clothes, and during the summers, I worked at a high-end boutique where I could get a large discount. I tried very hard not to excel at my studies, but somehow, no matter what I did, always came in third in my class. At school, I not only rebelled with the other students but was the first to do so. (In those days, the rebellions were political. We would decide not to open our books, for example, because there was rioting outside about the Baghdad Pact or the Suez War.)

My mother was clever. She never singled me out after these incidents; instead, she reprimanded the whole class. She knew that if she confronted me, our already strained relationship would become adversarial. But because she was anxious about my grades, she asked my aunt Salma to intervene. My aunt suggested that if I improved my grades and achieved first place, she would buy me a beautiful, expensive dress that I had seen and wanted, as a reward. This actually worked, but only briefly.

When I was seventeen, just two weeks before I was to attend the American University of Beirut, I learned that my mother had made the decision that I was to live in the college hostel, and not at my aunt's house, without consulting me. She had also decided, after speaking to the dean of women students at the university, that it would be good for me to do some work-study; they had agreed that running the cash register at the cafeteria, every morning, between 6 A.M. and 9 A.M., would be the right experience. I hit the roof, to no avail. But I quickly found a way out. I enrolled in 8 A.M. classes, which meant that I could not work the cash register, and quit the work-study program without my mother's knowledge. I spent my freshman year at the college hostel, but after that, my brothers and I decided to share an apartment in Beirut inside the family complex.

I was elated at the thought that my brothers and I would be living alone, and as the only female, I immediately took charge of decorating the place my way. My mother came by a couple of days later while we were at school. She looked around and decided that she did not like the way I arranged the furniture in the living room and proceeded to rearrange it. I came home and was beside myself when I saw what she had done. I put it back the way it had been. The next day, she did the same thing. This continued for weeks, until I finally got my way.

Our relationship improved after I graduated from college and became independent. I began to see her more often and got to know her better. We spent many hours talking. When I started to work, she discovered that I was good with money. She mentioned that my father had never asked her what she wanted to do with her paycheck. I told her that it was not Father's fault; it was hers, for not saying what she wanted to do with it. I sensed that she was asking for my help. I suggested that we open a joint account and that I would teach her how to use it— how to withdraw and deposit money. Father did not mind; how Mother used her money was not an issue with him. We did open an account together, and she began to be interested in it, reading her statements and trying hard to manage her money, but when I moved to the United States to study, she panicked and asked me to close it.

In the summer of 1970, I decided to marry Edward Said. Mother was delighted because he was a professor. They held similar political views and got along very well. What she did not like was that we would be living in the United States, far away. So before I knew it, she had convinced him to take a job at the Institute of Palestine Studies. She persuaded him to do this when he was visiting Beirut without me. When he came back, he seemed very excited about the prospect of taking the job, and our moving there. He did not even think of asking me whether I would like to move back. When I objected, he said, "I thought you would be happy living near your parents." I surprised him when I said that I preferred living in New York. Spending our summers in Beirut was enough for me. In fact, deep down, Edward was relieved. He did not want to leave his teaching job at Columbia University.

In 1971, Edward and I went to Beirut for the summer. Mother had prepared an apartment in the same building for us to live in. We had just arrived; I was pregnant with our first child, Wadie. We were exhausted and went to sleep right away. Very early the following morning, we received a call from a relative who was a doctor. He told us that my mother had collapsed and had been taken to the hospital. We rushed to the hospital, to learn that Mother had had a serious stroke and was in a coma. She just lay there, silent. I was shocked. I had never seen her this way before. It had never occurred to me that she could die. The doctors said that she might not recover. For three weeks, it was touch and go. But my father insisted that she had no intention of dying. He was right. She regained consciousness but was in the hospital for months. It took her over a year to recover. She resumed her work in 1972, but was never quite the same, and retired in 1974.

My parents had been planning to spend their last years in their house in Brummana. Mother was going to write and enjoy the garden and the tranquility of the place. But less than a year later, the civil war started. She later told me that this was the first time in her life that she was happy that her children were not around her.

Living through the civil war was extremely traumatic for her. She hated guns and was frightened of the people who carried them. At some point, it seemed that the country was going to be divided along religious lines. My parents lived in Ras Beirut, which was a mixed area, and became known as West Beirut during the war. The Christian coalition wanted to make sure that all the Christians relocated to East Beirut. To ensure that this took place, anonymous callers contacted families, and the voice on the other end of the phone would say, "We know exactly where you are. If you do not pack and leave by tomorrow, we will target you with our missiles." These calls paralyzed her. Once, the doorbell rang when she was alone at home with our deaf cook. It was an effort for her to get up. Before opening the door, she asked "Who is it?" "The superintendent," replied a voice. She recognized it and opened the door to find the superintendent as well as two bleeding men with machine guns. She was terrified when they mentioned my brother Nadim by name. She quickly composed herself and said, "Before you talk to me, put down your rifles." (What rifles? They had sophisticated machine guns!) But they put down their machine guns. Then they explained to her that they had been told that a doctor named Nadim lived there (my brother was a doctor), and they needed medical help because they had been shot. She was relieved. At the time, gunmen were entering homes, looting and killing innocent people. Many a night was spent in corridors and in shelters when the indiscriminate shelling was going on.

I visited Lebanon with my children, Wadie and Najla, during a brief lull in the war in 1977. My father took us to see devastated downtown Beirut. My mother refused to come. Later, she asked Wadie, "What did you see?" He was five years old. He said, "A big broken city."

I last saw my mother in the summer of 1978. I noticed that she had aged and that her movements were slower. She was exhausted with the war.

Edward visited her in March of 1979. Before leaving, my mother gave him the manuscript of her memoir and asked him to find a publisher for it in the United States. A few months later, my father came to see us in New York. My mother had not been able to travel since her stroke and never saw me in my home. She passed away, in her sleep, while he was visiting me.

To many in my mother's generation, Lebanon was a made-up country, largely invented by the French. My mother had grown up under Ottoman rule in Beirut, Syria. After World War I, the region was carved up by the colonial powers, and her country became a French mandate territory. The Middle East that emerged after World War I was composed of several countries that seemed precarious to her. During World War II, when she got married, Syria was divided into two independent countries, Syria and Lebanon, with Beirut as the capital of Lebanon. Its constitution was written by the French and was based on a division of power that attempted to balance the many religious sects that made up the population. This structure disturbed my mother, who was a secularist. My brothers and I grew up in a time of further political instability and upheaval in the area, as a result of 1948 when Palestine ceased to exist and Israel was created.

The Lebanese government could not withstand the many tensions and pressures that the Arab world experienced after 1948, which culminated in a mini–civil war in the summer of 1958 that lasted for a few months. My mother was extremely shaken by what was happening to the country. Though she had been recording her experiences since she was a teenager, she decided to write her memoir at this time.

The first edition of her book came out in Arabic, in the early 1960s, with the (same) title, *Dunia Ahbabtuha* (A World I Loved). It covered the period between 1917 and 1957. It was well received and became a popular textbook in schools, because it beautifully conveyed a part of the past that had been forgotten—a lost world.

A few years after it was published, the region became engulfed in continuous conflict and war. The first shock came in June 1967 when the so-called Six Day War took place and the Israelis occupied the rest of Palestine—the West Bank and Gaza Strip. Soon after the 1967 war, the Palestinians organized themselves into a resistance movement, the Palestine Liberation Organization (PLO) and began to gain prominence in the Arab world. This led to inter-Arab conflicts and a major confrontation between the Palestinians and the Jordanians in 1970, with the result that the PLO was thrown out of Jordan. That same year, in September, Gamal Abdel Nasser, the president of Egypt and the most prominent Arab leader since the early 1950s, died unexpectedly. His death was another shock the Arab world could not withstand: Nasser's successor, Anwar Sadat, proceeded to engage in another war with the Israelis in 1973, and more turbulence and instability occurred. A few years later, the Lebanese civil war started. My mother endured three and a half years of it. Then, in 1977, there was a hiatus, and they began to hope for better days. But the fighting erupted again, and in the spring of 1978, the Israelis invaded southern Lebanon. The civil war lasted fifteen long years. It was a horrible, brutal war that devastated the country, traumatized its population, and produced 150,000 deaths.

After she retired, friends and family encouraged my mother to revise and update her memoir, especially since the Lebanese civil war was slowly obliterating the country. Though frail and in some ways incapacitated, she proceeded to edit the first edition and to write a whole new section, covering the years from 1957 to 1977. My mother died soon after she finished writing and editing it, and never saw the final product. The second Arabic edition was published posthumously in 1982.

The first edition of my mother's book sold out in the 1960s, and strange as it may seem, no one—not my father, brothers, relatives, or myself—had a copy. My mother's personal copies disappeared during the many moves my parents endured during the civil war. The editions in the school library were destroyed when the building was shelled. The original publisher had ceased to exist. Considering the state of chaos in Lebanon, this seemed normal. However, strange things do happen. Soon after the U.S. invasion of Iraq in 2003, a distant relative of mine happened to be in Baghdad. He was browsing in a bookstore and saw a copy. He picked up the book, read the dedication, and saw my mother's name. How bizarre and surreal it was to find Wadad Khuri-Makdisi's out-of-print memoir in war-torn Baghdad in 2003. He bought it and gave it to my brother, who generously made photocopies of the book, bound them, and gave a copy to each of us—my brothers, my innumerable cousins, and me.

Before her stroke, my mother was also working on another version of the book, written directly in English, which she completed after she recovered. It is the version that is published here today. She felt compelled to write it in English to explain to the West the politics around the Palestinian tragedy that had unfolded in the region. It was meant to be a testimony to that largely unknown history.

This book is the manuscript she gave to my husband, Edward. He read it and gave it to several friends and editors. But the book was long and needed editing; it was written in a picaresque style and contained many descriptions of her travels in the Arab world. No publisher was interested in what seemed a remote narrative.

Then 9/11 happened. It changed many things. The war on terror, Islam, the occupation of Afghanistan, and the invasion of Iraq, all became the issues of the day. It seemed that the time for her book had come.

It is interesting to note my mother's omissions in the memoir. As a woman who grew up in the Arab world, she was taught not to boast, but to speak of herself as part of a whole—a community or a nation. She was so conscious of this that she went out of her way not to say that Edward Said was her son-in-law and refers to him only as "the scholar Edward Said." Nor would one know that Constantin Zurayk, the distinguished professor at the American University of Beirut, and a famous Arab historian, who wrote 'Ma'na al Nakba'—The Meaning of Catastrophe— and coined the term Al-Nakba, was her brother-in-law, married to my father's sister. In the book, she mentions that she secretly read the writings of a relative who lived in Manchester, England. That relative was Albert Hourani, the well-known professor at Oxford, and the author of The History of the Arab Peoples.

Nor does she mention her many achievements. She speaks of Alexis Boutros, the conductor, as a man who needed a place in which to rehearse choral music—she had offered her school— and notes that her students had participated. What she omits is just how hard she worked to convince the parents of the girls at her school that choral music was a respectable endeavor and that music, itself, was an important part of education. To this end, she gave a passionate talk on the radio, urging the parents to allow it. The press covered her talk; she succeeded.

She was also instrumental in establishing the Academie Libanaise des Beaux Arts, currently part of the University of Bala- mand, with Boutros and a group of intellectuals. The Academie Libanaise was the first private Lebanese institution of higher learning in which the arts—dance, music, and architecture—were taught. She was on its board and served as its secretary for many years. This job was practically another full-time endeavor.

She was a member of many institutional boards, including Asfurieh, a mental health institute; Brummana High School, the Quaker school my brothers attended; and the Institute of Palestinian Studies, among others.

She was very politically active. Before Lebanon gained independence, she, like many others, belonged to committees and societies that were working toward autonomy. In 1941, to prevent a takeover of Lebanon and Syria by the Vichy government in France, the British Army and the Free French invaded Lebanon. At that point General Charles de Gaulle came to Lebanon and claimed it as Free French territory. My mother marched along with men and women of all sects and religions to demand Lebanon's independence.

Although she was the headmistress of a private school, she was a strong believer in public education. She did what she could to elevate the standards of Lebanese public schools. She was an adviser at some point to the Ministry of Education and tried very hard to improve the public school curriculum.

She also belonged to a group of emancipated secular Lebanese women, of all sects and religions, who lobbied for the rights of women. In the 1950s, they fought for the right to vote and won. But many of the laws needed to be modified to make women equal citizens in the fuller sense. The group demanded that the law of inheritance be changed so that women could inherit the same share as men. Here, they partially succeeded. The law was modified, but only for non-Muslim women. Even today, a Muslim woman's inheritance is based on the Sharia, not secular law. Another law stated that permission from a male relative was required if a woman wanted to travel. A passport could not be issued without this written consent. The law was changed during the civil war. It had annoyed my mother when she was traveling with a group of students. The fathers had to give her power of attorney, stating that they designated her as the guardian of their children. These letters had to be presented to the passport office, and my mother had to sign for each applicant before they could receive their passports. Finally, after signing for thirty students, she presented her own passport for renewal. The clerk looked at her, smiled, and said, "I need your husband's written permission." She couldn't believe the twisted logic. Women were also not allowed to own a business. After years of protest against it, this law was recently changed. But alas, not all of the laws have been modified to allow equality in every sphere. Women still cannot bestow Lebanese citizenship on their children.

One of the role models in my mother's life was her aunt Amina, her father's sister, who never married and founded and ran a school. As children, we used to hear this story about her: Once, sometime before World War I, Amina went to visit a mosque with my grandfather and some of his friends. She was the only woman in the group. When they got to the mosque, the guard said to her, "You cannot go up to the minaret." She asked, "Why not?" He answered, "God gave you half a brain and made you inherit half a man's share." She looked at him, straight in the eye, and said, "God gave me a full brain, and it is men like you who gave me half the inheritance." She turned and proceeded to climb up the stairs to the minaret.

I find it amazing that some of what she and my mother fought for, so many years ago, is still being debated today.

I

~

THIS IS MY STORY, the story of an Arab woman. It is the story of a lost world. It begins in 1917, in Syria, when I was seven years old. War hung heavy over us at that time, and yet I had a happy childhood, this owing to the serenity of my parents and the luxury of innocence. I was a middle child in a family of three girls and three boys, and if there is one thing that brought us all unscarred through those years, it was a sense of gratitude, even for the small things in life.

We grew up in Beirut, a city by the sea.[1] The city itself was a small, unsophisticated town then. Perhaps it was the modesty of the place or the ordinary affinities of childhood; whatever the reason, for me the city's treasure was its situation in the natural world and, as I learned from my father's stories, in history as well. On hot summer days Father often accompanied us along narrow sandy lanes lined with cactus hedges down to the beach. Swimming was a delight, made more so because few other youngsters were allowed to enjoy this particular pleasure at that time. When it was too cold to swim, we followed the rocky coastline into the harbor area, watching the boats and playing a geography game, naming the gigantic rocks in the distance for

islands of the Mediterranean: the nearest to us, Cyprus; the far-
thest, Malta; another, Crete. In the bay small boats bore oranges and tangerines from Haifa and Jaffa, or sugar cane and
lemons from Sidon and Tyre. There were passenger ships, too,
from Alexandria, which made short stops and then sailed on to
the Turkish, Greek, and Italian harbors. As we watched, Father
would remind us that these waters had once welcomed Egyptian and Phoenician triremes, which had roamed the seas trading
purple cloth and gold jewelry, and Roman and Byzantine galleys, which had brought warriors. He told us legends, too, of
Neptune and St. George, the lore of centuries past, of civiliza-
tions that left their mark on our shores and their secrets buried
in the sea.

We learned to love the sea in all of its moods: when its
mighty waves broke against the rocks, when its tides crept in
during the silent nights, when it was a calm, deep blue, reflecting the dome of the sky. Perhaps the fisherman Khalil knew its
moods better than anyone. He was too poor to buy a boat, so
he spent most of his sixty years perched on rocks, patiently
waiting. Year after year he toiled and waited. Even the fierce
storms of winter, for him the unkindest season, were no deterrent. On the eve of World War I, when an Italian battleship
bombarded the Lebanese coast and most of the people had fled
to the hills, Khalil remained. He was confident that nothing
would befall him, as nothing had befallen his father when he
saw Napoleon and the British fight at Acre. "Now the Turks are
here, and the Europeans are coming to drive them away," he
said. "We don't know who may come next. Conquerors come
and go. Only the sea is eternally with us."

My girlhood memories are populated by those like Khalil—
fishermen, tradesmen, and tinkers, the laborers who kept the
town going. I can still remember the shoe mender, with his roll

of thick leather and his portable cobbler's kit; the brazier, who retinned our brass kitchen utensils; the knife sharpener, who ambled down the street with his large wheel, singing his trade tune. The streets vibrated with such songs. The plant seller chanted while riding a donkey and balancing heaps of flowers on his saddle. The goatherd drove his black goats through now fashionable neighborhoods, his call rising above the faint clanging of the bells that swung from around their necks. Our next-door neighbor, Hassan, a man of sixty, sold nut-sweets and spent his whole life walking the streets in a long white robe with a tray on his head, singing.

Not far from our house, in what were called the Hamra fields, stood an old mosque. From its minaret, illuminated at night by candles, the muezzin sounded the call to prayer five times a day, his voice fading into its own echo. Not far from the mosque, mulberry trees stretched into the fields by the hundreds. Our neighbors had a silkworm farm. Rows of elevated twig racks held large trays of reed and upon those were heaped the silkworms, which fed on mulberry leaves until they began to spin their cocoons. After harvest the piles of gleaming white cocoons were softened in boiling water and then slowly unraveled to make spools of thread. After the war artificial silk was imported, the factories went out of business, and the mulberry trees were replaced by banana and orange orchards.

We would not have thought it then, but the war brought the twentieth century to Beirut. Those who gave a certain rhythm to our daily life—the potters propelling their wheels by foot amid the fragrance of wet clay; the neighborhood blacksmith and his two boys, deaf from typhus, who helped in the shop but whose great talent was kite-making; the baker, who didn't make and sell bread at all but rather baked the prepared dough that the people, without ovens, brought him; the blind man who roamed the streets singing for alms until he learned to mend chairs, at which point he had two occupations—all of those people belonged to another time.

So, in more than one sense, did our childhood. My father was a professor of Arabic at what is now known as the American University of Beirut. He had a heady optimism and a keen sense of humor. He had grown up in the mountains overlooking the coastal city of Tripoli and at sixteen took off with a mule caravan, along the hazardous coast, to Beirut for an education. The American University was then called Syrian Protestant College, and he worked his way through, planting trees and translating books into Arabic for rural schools.[2] Years after graduation, he returned to teach. He had a passion for folk stories from Arab history and a wonderful gift for relating these simple tales with wit and style. In 1909 he began publishing a quarterly cultural magazine called *Clear Spring*, and thanks to that journalistic venture, more than twenty periodicals came to us regularly from Cairo, Damascus, Jerusalem, and Tunisia.

My mother was a gentle, unassuming person who had no feminine vanities. She was small, with a serene face and dark hair parted in the middle, revealing a large forehead. Mother's bliss was to devote herself completely to the comfort of her family. That, and the health of her garden. Although she lived most of her life in a city, she remained a true product of the countryside, where nature was considered as precious as human beings. During winter storms, when thunder seemed to shake the whole of creation and the rains made rivers of the streets, Mother worried about everything. She worried about the neighbors, whose house was low and poorly built, about people in the nearby street who lived in miserable shacks with no blankets or covers, about the trees in her garden with which the winds played havoc. Every need aroused her tenderness, and it greatly disturbed her conscience that she was unable to ease suffering more. To Father the winds were a challenge. How often he insisted that we go with him for walks in winter! Wrapped in a thick camel-skin aba, with a red tarboosh on his head and a strong oak cane in his hand, he would stand through the tempest by the sea. I think the violent bellows brought out the defiance in him and stimulated his imagination.

We lived in a beautiful old house on what is now Jeanne D'Arc Street, in the Ras-Beirut neighborhood. My mother's garden was spacious and protected by a cactus hedge. The garden walks of hard-packed earth were shaded by fig, olive, lemon, and bitter orange trees, whose heavy fragrance filled the air in spring. In the center was a pool shaded by vine and white jasmine; to the left, eucalyptus and white-blossomed oleander. Mother grew some vegetables, but mostly flowers—roses and carnations, masses of white marguerites, violets, lilies, and red and white geraniums. The house was built around an airy reception hall, its oak-beam ceiling five meters high. Three doors on each side of this hall opened onto adjacent rooms. Persian carpets covered the floor of the drawing room, and a small harmonium, Father's wedding gift to Mother, anchored one corner. We rarely spent our evenings there, though, preferring the dining room, a warm setting for games and discussion of the day's events.

Of all the rooms in the house, Father's was the most alluring. On one wall hung a poster of famous men in history: Adam, followed by his progeny—Moses, David, Ramses, Hippocrates, Avecinna, Galileo, Columbus, Napoleon, Pasteur. They all had long beards and penetrating eyes. Opposite this hung a map of the heavens. We would sit beside Father on the edge of the bed learning to identify the Big Bear, the Little Bear, the Gemini twins, ferocious Leo, mighty Centaurus and his Lupus, Taurus, and Capricorn. Mother's room had no decoration except a simple reproduction of Christ at Gethsemane. Next to her bed was a cot for my youngest brother, and on the nearby sofa was a large sewing basket full of stockings, which she would pick up after we had been tucked into bed, darning into the late hours by the dim light of a kerosene lamp.

At the entrance to the house was a grand arched porch. Father would recline there to read while we played around him, our exuberance an apparent source of delight to him. Our favorite playground, though, was the campus of the American University. This was a world of wonders. Trees of every height and shape spread their welcoming shade—cypresses and palms, fruit trees and ancient olives, the dangling fig, the climbing honeysuckle. In the summer carob trees bore their sweet brown pods, reminding us of the story of the Prodigal Son, who ate carob husks while tending the swine. Oleanders, mimosas, and hibiscus framed the views of the bay and the mountains, all blues and purples fringed in white, red, and yellow. At the entrance to the chapel stood a colossal banyan tree. Best of all were a few specimens of the cedars of Lebanon.

The university had a natural history museum with many stuffed creatures in glass cases. Desert owls and eagles, birds of all kinds, posed in sand or perched on twigs. A baby elephant from Africa, a beautiful zebra, two foxes, and a white bear drew our special attention, though none thrilled us so much as the Arabian horses and the desert gazelles. Not far from the museum stood broken statues and columns, ruins of the Phoenicians and Romans. To the west a great part of the campus was wild with thorns growing in ferocious disharmony. Cyclamen flamed up from underneath the rocks; daisies, red and violet anemones, poppies, and white lilies bloomed in gay patches. To the east, overlooking the sea, was an amphitheater on whose cold seats we often sat for vespers as the sun vanished beneath the horizon, coloring the coastline and beyond to the heights. On clear summer nights we tested our knowledge of the stars. Only once were we given the chance to gaze through the huge telescope in the university observatory. We saw mountains on the moon; we saw the shining rings of Saturn.

In this radiant world we played through the changing seasons of our childhood.

II

~

M Y FIRST ACQUAINTANCE with grief came one day on a
visit with my father to the Hamra Mosque. An old
sheikh guarded its entrance. He had a great many stories of
saints and prophets, which, like much Oriental literature, had
been transmitted to him orally. Worried that his friend might
not live long enough to reveal the priceless store of his memory, Father visited with him daily, returning stocked with new
tales and anecdotes. (Although nurtured in Christian tradition, my father's spiritual and literary interests knew no limi-
tation of creed.) We children would come along whenever we
had the chance, and on this particular morning the sheikh was
disturbed.

"Two sons have met their death at the battlefront," the
sheikh murmured. They had been fighting, he said, in Dara,
Syria. "Give me strength, my Lord, to accept my fate with
courageous surrender." When we returned home, Father made
me write that verse for him in one of the little diaries I kept. It
would take me years to understand what it really meant. The
fate of the sheikh's sons was not uncommon. While tilling the
fields, our neighbor's only son was taken away to join the Turk-

ish army. His family was not allowed even to bid him goodbye. Luckier young men boarded the last boat to the United States.

Others had different dreams. On May 6, 1916, the Ottoman governor, Jamal Pacha, had ordered the execution of more than twenty Lebanese and Syrian leaders who, with an aim toward independence, had been in contact with Europe. The executions took place simultaneously in Damascus and Beirut. The Arab world had been reluctant to oppose the Turks, but when Jamal Pacha ignored entreaties for mercy from the Hashemite Prince Faisal, the Arab Revolt was declared. Young Arabs fought at the side of the Allies in the hope of obtaining self-government.

Father was initially skeptical about the good of all this fighting and about the promises of the Western powers. The spring and summer of 1917 were weighted with suffering. Half-naked people, hopeless and hungry, walked the streets of Beirut begging for scraps of bread, searching through garbage. Babies cried incessantly. No longer allowed to go downtown or to the sea, we played in our garden or in our campus world, as our parents tried to protect us from the sharpest impact of those days. Their care could not, however, shut out the sights we saw or the sound of wailing that came to us at night while we were in bed. The Turks and Germans needed every provision for their armies, so there was little left for the people.

Hatred toward Jamal Pacha was boundless. In retrospect, it may have been our family's salvation. Once, in Jerusalem, he was hit in the jaw by a bullet. A clever British dental specialist from the American University of Beirut performed an operation, the success of which gave the governor renewed appreciation for the institution. He allowed it to remain open, recognizing also that it could be useful in training doctors for the Turkish army. The entire university and its staff were granted rations of flour. Thus it was that, although we lacked many basic foods, we had enough to survive.

As the action of the war neared Beirut in July of 1917, we left for a quiet part of the mountains. We rode off early one morning in a cart drawn by two mules loaded with our belongings, my father and eldest brother walking alongside. Here and there in the hills we found villages deserted and partly demolished, the houses' supporting beams having been sold for bread. Many times we stopped to drink from roadside fountains and looked back to see Beirut enfolded in mist. The Mediterranean faded from view as the red-tiled roofs and verdant pines of Dhour el-Shoueir drew nearer.

We would spend two summers there, and soon enough Father would come to speak of "the Great War." People were dying of starvation, especially in the mountain areas, but the Turkish army along with the Germans were in a desperate fight. The British were in Jerusalem by December of 1917. The city had offered little resistance, and the population hailed the Europeans as liberators. They soon headed toward Dara, on their way to Damascus, to liberate the rest of Syria.

Those who did not live in that time can never know the wonder, even for a child, of the news of the liberation of the Holy City. This signal event occurred on December 9, but because we had no radio or regular cables, word of it took more than a week to reach us. Father gathered all of the press material, then recounted for us how the cavalry had entered Jerusalem as the Arab armies advanced toward its gates. Although Father gave credit to the Allied forces, especially Britain's Gen. Edmund Allenby and his troops, his hopes were set on Prince Faisal, son of Sharif Hussein, who led the Arab forces. Like all Arab nationalists of the time, Father dreamed of an undivided Syria, the boundaries of which included the autonomous Mount Lebanon region and Palestine. Such ideas were not limited to Arabs. Howard Bliss, president of the American University, was also deeply interested in the independence of Arab lands and greatly admired Prince Faisal.

It was not so much news of war that inflamed our childish imagination as our father's stories of the golden city of Jerusalem. He told us of the Caliph Omar the Pious, who in the seventh century came from Medina to free the city from the Byzantines. When invited to enter a Christian church for prayer, Caliph Omar was said to have knelt down in the open courtyard and announced his covenant with the city's inhabitants: "In tolerance and peace men of all faiths must live here forevermore." We learned, too, of the great Saladin, who took the city from the Crusaders in the twelfth century and was generous to his enemies. He was reputed to have reminded his men after the battle: "O Servants of God, let not Satan deceive you that Victory was due to your swords; Victory comes only from Him."

There was a family story as well. As I remember it, from my father's telling it went something like this. My great-grandfather Saba Khoury was a grain merchant who learned to read and write between the ages of twenty-five and thirty and eventually became a Greek Orthodox priest. He continued to be a grain trader as well, and in 1848 he contracted cholera during an epidemic and died. (The tablet on his tomb is still venerated as a healing spot by the villagers in the region of Akkar, Syria.)[1] His son, my grandfather, who gave the family his name—Makdisi, which means "Jerusalem pilgrim"—refused to become a priest but was the first of his clan to make the pilgrimage to the Holy City. This was probably around 1858. He rode a mule from Tripoli, traveling along the coast road to Beirut, Sidon, Tyre, Haifa, and Jaffa, from whence he carried on to Jerusalem. It must have taken him more than a fortnight, sleeping in shabby

monasteries, buying frugal provisions along the way. He probably lingered there through the winter, joining other pilgrims on
the return home in the spring. In May he reached Damascus,
and from there he trekked to his village in the Akkar region. As
his neighbors, possibly a crowd of one hundred, chanted their
song of welcome, he sprinkled sand from the Holy Land on
their doorsteps; on Sunday he poured water from the Jordan
River into the baptismal basin. His pilgrimage was the life
dream of every believer.

The liberation of Jerusalem thus became another scene in the
sequence of ancient history, family history, and war news that
formed the story of our early lives. We left Dhour el-Shoueir and
returned to Beirut in the fall of 1918, just as the Allies were declaring victory. Germans and Turks were streaming out of the
city as the British army marched in from the Sidon road. Everyone was rejoicing; in the mountains, fires were lit in celebration.
It seemed the day of independence had arrived. A ten-year-old
American girl we knew wrote a naïve verse in honor of the event:

> On October first, the year 1918,
> A wonderful sight in our village was seen:
> Guns popping, flags flying, sky rockets went up:
> We were so excited we hardly could sup:
> The Turks had all left us, the British were near:
> Our troubles were over, we knew peace was here.
> Hurrah for the Arab nations—three cheers!
> Away with all sorrow and sighing and tears:
> The people are happy because they all know
> That their Arab nation in freedom may grow.

III

∾

W<small>HEN THE ARMISTICE</small> was signed, on November 11, the
schools had a holiday. Scots Highlanders paraded in
their colorful kilts, marching with their bands through the main
streets of Beirut. With the Scotsmen and the British came the
Arab forces who had led them through the desert, the Egyptians
with their humorous songs, as well as Indians, South Africans,
Australians, and Canadians. With the French came the Algerians, the Senegalese, and the Indo-Chinese. It was a joyous time,
and then it was not.

All through the winter of 1918, my father's university colleagues gathered at home and spoke late into the evening. My
parents' house typically received a parade of visitors. The ladies
of our community had regular reception days; my mother's was
Thursday. As for my father, I think there was not a day in the
whole year when he did not receive guests. As I grew older I
took increasing interest in the talk that went around—the
charming proverbial expressions of the simpler guests, the news
of newlyweds and newborns, of bad marriages and lucky
matches, of home and the world, life's expectations and
tragedies small and large.

Uncle Dumit was Father's most regular visitor. Well versed in Arabic culture, an authority on linguistics, he would exchange newspapers and magazines, most of them from Egypt, as well as opinions with my father. When the war started, the eldest of his six children was sent to the United States to escape military service. The second enlisted in the Turkish army but was never exposed to danger. Uncle Dumit supported the Turks. He maintained that it would be easier for the Arabs to unite under a weak Turkey than to seek a new ally. The Turks are unable to control their vast empire, he argued; they would be glad to let us take care of ourselves. Britain and France are greedy and ambitious, he said. They have interests contrary to ours. Why trust them at all?

During the war my father and many of his other guests held different views. They were cosmopolitans. Father's closest colleague was the Dutchman Van Dyke, a great scientist who spoke Arabic, savored Father's stories of Arab culture, and attempted to write in our language. Another colleague, Uncle Kurban, had nine children dispersed throughout the world, the most brilliant of whom revived a movement of Arabic literature and taught in Brazil. Dr. Atiyeh, a popular physician, had spent most of his life in the service of the British in Sudan. His only son was granted a scholarship to Oxford, which the boy accepted only after the whole community convinced his mother that the opportunity was worth their separation. There was Michalany, a retired high-ranking official of the British government, formerly stationed in Egypt. There was President Bliss, of the university, and his wife. And there was an Armenian family, which became acquainted with both of my parents. The father, an amateur archaeologist, had a store in town that was the first to sell photographic equipment, greeting cards, and Christmas decorations. The seven children were our playmates, but I was fascinated most by the grandmother, who at the age of six had left her parents in their remote Asia Minor town and attended boarding school in Jaffa.

The comings and goings of such people was so regular as to be generally unremarkable, but one night some intimate friends assembled in our house, speaking in low voices and with deep distress. Just that morning Father had been full of enthusiasm as he left the house to attend the hoisting of the new Arab flag. When he came home, there was a sadness about him. He laid a small flag on the table without looking at us, almost deaf to our questions. As we rushed in excitement to raise the flag on top of the garden gate, he called us back. "Keep it in the house," he said. "Hoist it anywhere you wish, but do not expose it to the main street."

During the last days of the war the Arab flag had been a subject of special joy for my father. Now his words left us speechless. The next morning Uncle Dumit sat with us at breakfast. It turned out that no sooner had the Arab flag been raised than the British and French ordered it to be removed. Although the Arabs had been promised independence, secret agreements had been worked out by the great powers to divide the conquered Ottoman territories. "Did I not tell you that the British and French are against us?" Uncle Dumit said. "Thousands of Arabs have died to help them enter the country. Many of our young men were hanged because they gave them their help. Mark my words: they will stab us in the back."

Many of my father's colleagues became indignant that Sharif Hussein had trusted the Allies. The Arab Revolt had won the war for the Allies over the Turks. Now the Balfour Declaration, with its commitment of British support for a Jewish "national home" in Palestine, and the Sykes-Picot Agreement, which drew borders designating our land as French or British colonial territory, were devised to destroy Arab unity and foreclose independence. "These are devilish and shameful documents!" Uncle Dumit said.

Still, Father continued to believe that America would lend a hand, and for some time our forebodings vied with our hopes. The years passed, but Father maintained high expectations for Arab unity. On March 20, 1920, Prince Faisal was proclaimed king over an undivided Syria, including Palestine. Celebrations took place in Damascus and Beirut. But one hot day in July, news came that the French had savagely attacked the Arab legion of the new king. I can still remember the grief in Father's voice when he told us. The beautiful city of Damascus had been bombarded. The king had fled. Rumors spread that he was in Baghdad.

Our fate was to be decided at a peace conference in Paris. Howard Bliss pleaded for the Arab cause, but no one listened to him. Even the American president, Woodrow Wilson, was out of the picture. France laid her hand on Syria and demarcated Lebanon as a separate country, now including the coastal cities of Tripoli, Beirut, Sidon, and Tyre, as well as the mountain districts. Britain took over Iraq and Palestine. Egypt and Sudan were to stay under British tutelage. Promises of Arab freedom seemed infinitely deferred. The seeds were sown for Arab distrust of the West. The British attacked Iraq, using gas shells and ordinary bombs. Some in England opposed the use of gas, but Winston Churchill, then secretary of state at the War Office, called them squeamish; such chemical agents, he said, "would spread a lively terror." In 1921 the British allowed King Faisal to sit on the throne in Baghdad. They gave his brother Abdullah a desert emirate that they carved out of eastern Palestine and named Transjordan. No one knew exactly what awaited the rest of Palestine, which by that stroke had been reduced to less than a quarter of its former size. Father was in despair when he learned that the first high commissioner of Palestine was a British Zionist. He felt more saddened when Hebrew was declared one of its three official languages. Even the small minority of Jews who lived in Palestine then, and who formed about 12 percent of the population, spoke mostly Arabic among themselves. Riots and panic became the order of the day. Suspicion was everywhere. A period of hatred and despair was descending.

IV

&

FOUR YEARS OF WAR had made it impossible for us to have contact with my mother's family, so in the summer of 1920 Father decided to take us to northern Lebanon to visit our grandparents. We rode in a simple horse-drawn coach, a canvas canopy swaying over our heads, along the Phoenician coast, past the orchards of Antilias with their oranges and almonds. The route we took was ancient. In the gorge where the Dog River empties into the sea and the mountains press close to the rocky shore, Father pointed out chariot ruts worn deep into the rock, traces of a Roman road. Thousands of years ago an Assyrian king led his army over this route, and as they paused by the river, they left an inscription on the cliff, telling posterity that here had passed the conquering army of Nebuchadnezzar. The proud king established a precedent. The armies of Ramses II, the Roman legions, Napoleon III, and the British Expeditionary Force of 1918 under General Allenby all left inscriptions on the cliffs. We got out of the coach and climbed the rocky hillside to identify them. We counted fifteen; more would be added. Father did not live to see the last of them, made by French troops in 1946 as they evacuated from our territories.

We left the river gorge and moved on to the great curving bay of Junieh, the heights crowned with a statue of the Madonna. The town was almost deserted. Children and widows roamed the narrow streets. Most of the young men had fled abroad. Some had died of famine and disease. We pressed on to the Adonis River. Under willow trees by its banks we had a lunch of river fish, fried over a blazing fire, while Father entertained us with the story of Astarte, the Phoenician Venus who fell in love with Adonis: "One day she lost sight of him, and she rode over the hills in her swan-drawn chariot. How miserable she became upon discovering that he had been attacked by a ferocious bear. Her tears fell on the grass while his blood ran into the river, changing its color to red."

Because Father insisted on stopping at every interesting turn, it would be sunset before we reached Byblos, and thus the following day before we explored the place. That morning was fresh with the fragrance of late spring. The extensive ruins of Byblos had not yet been unearthed; as we walked with Father along the shore, only the aged castle could be seen at a distance. Fragments of weathered walls and pillars were strewn about the grassy mounds. Near the citadel, British bombs had left their scars on the Crusaders' church, but upon entering we found lit candles and holy oil and, along its walls, an abundance of damaged saints. Father was more interested in talking about ancient Byblos, though. We looked out upon the broad sea imagining Egyptian galleys laden with treasures, envisioning ships carrying timber and hundreds of masons from here to Tyre and then to Jerusalem to build the temple of Solomon. On a subsequent holiday to the north, we would climb the slopes of the highest range in Lebanon, deforested by the Phoenician king for the sake of that temple, and we would step into the deep shade of the awesome cedar grove. But that would be years later; for now we had our father's word pictures.

Back in the coach heading north, we saw men here and there gathering salt in rocky pools along the coast. A few boats were anchored in the haven of Tabarja. "From this modest bay St. Peter sailed to Rome," Father informed us, quickly adding, "but St. Paul preferred the grand harbor of Antioch." On the Tripoli road, as the horses plodded along the edge of a monstrous sheer cliff, Father's travelogue conjured scenes of frightened horses rearing up out of control, falling off the rocky ledges to the sea below and dragging their riders with them. We rode along safely, in a state of high excitement. Ahead lay the quiet villages of Enfeh and Chekka. The rich cement of their hills had not yet been discovered. People still survived off the small salt ponds that had been carved in the rocks by the sea. The frowning ravines seemed endless as our horses climbed on. Another three hours of riding, and the green hills of Kura opened onto vineyards. As our coach approached the center of the village of Bterram, people flocked to greet us. Before long, we were resting on the shaded veranda of my grandmother's house, sipping grenadine juice cooled with mountain snow.

In our grandparents' orchard, almonds, hawthorns, walnuts, quince, pears, and apples grew in abundance. A huge olive tree shaded a cistern, where rainwater was kept for the dry summer days. Every home had cistern water for household uses, but the village people drank from a nearby fountain. At sunset the way to the fountain was filled with laughing women, their bright dresses swaying in the evening breeze. Admiring young men watched as they strolled by. Many a love match was born along that fountain road.

My grandfather was the village doctor and pharmacist. Often he would ride his donkey down the coast to Tripoli, where he would spend hours poring over medical manuscripts. Sometimes he paid as much as one gold pound to borrow a document, then copied it by hand through the night. I remember watching him put drops in the eyes of the aged, prepare herbs or quinine pills for malaria patients, or calm the fears of an anxious mother whose child had convulsed in the night. A year or two after our visit, a doctor fully trained in modern medicine came to the village. Grandfather's sight was failing. The villagers, however, went on drinking his herbs and taking his quinine pills unmindful of the other doctor.

My grandmother had a serious look, though her eyes were weak; she was tall but stooped. Of her children, only two daughters remained in the village. Five sons had immigrated to the United States, Australia, and Haiti. Another was in Beirut, where he was my father's colleague at the American University. Both of my grandparents were generous-spirited. If my grandfather chanced to see passersby picking his grapes or figs, he averted his eyes. People spoke of my grandmother as the woman who could not sleep if she heard that someone was hungry, and she always cooked enough so that there was plenty to share. Grandmother taught us to make use of every little bit of a thing. Grapes that were not fit for raisins were dipped into a jar to become vinegar. Olive seeds were gathered for winter fuel; the crude oil was made into soap.

We spent a great deal of time watching village people at work. Women sat on the floor making large thin sheets of dough, then baking those in primitive stoves on hot convex trays of iron, feeding the fire with thistles from the fields. In a minute or two the delicate sheet was baked through and carefully peeled off to make room for the next. Women walked barefoot up the hillside gathering fuel for these fires. One young mother was cut doing this. Within days she was dead of blood poisoning, leaving a family of small children to mourn her.

In the hot month of August we were allowed to sleep in the vineyard. Our little arbor was built up on high poles and constructed of dry oak branches and leaves. A long ladder led up to the wooden floor where our beds were laid on bare planks. We shared our knowledge of the planets and constellations with the village children. Most of them were ordinarily too pinned down by hard living to look up at the stars for long.

Nearly every Sunday a saint's day festivity took place in a church or convent in my grandparents' village. It seemed to us that all the saints chose to be born in the summer. These celebrations of the Eastern Orthodox Church were feasts for the senses. I remember mighty young men pulling on the ropes of the church bell as it resounded in the fields and valleys, the priest's mantle glittering with golden embroidery, and the crown of jewels on his head. I remember the chanted prayers, the youngsters bearing weighty candlesticks and walking in rhythm round the priest, the click of his censer and the smoke suffusing the air with fragrance, the crystal lamp scattering light on icons of the Virgin and the saints, and at the end the deep rich sound of the bell once more. After the Mass families gathered in the courtyard, preparing small fires and grilling fresh meat. There was gaiety and laughter, the sharing of food, folk tunes, and dances.

Baptisms and weddings also took place in the village church. The latter were the more exciting of the two, stretching as they did long into the night. An important wedding festival once lasted more than ten days. On such occasions people seemed to forget the miseries from the war. Although most of the old women wore formal black, young girls dressed in brilliant costumes made from the new artificial silk that was coming into the country. As colorful as that fabric was, my grandmother lamented the passing of the silk factories. "Hundreds of village girls found their livelihood in them," she said. "How sad it is that we cannot weave our own clothes anymore."

We bid goodbye to my maternal grandparents and headed for Tripoli to visit my father's family. Father's people, originally from the Syrian highlands, had migrated south with the seasons. His father had settled in the city of Homs, in northern Syria, and later moved his family of seven children to Tripoli, where he aimed to educate them. When they came of age, some of his sons sought their future in the United States. My father and his youngest brother, Uncle Anis, went to Beirut.

During our youth Uncle Anis was the most popular figure in the family. Good-looking and energetic, imaginative by nature, he wrote patriotic and romantic poetry. He was known as "the river poet" for his verses inspired by our region's historic waterways. But he also wrote fiery poems calling for Arab unity, which the youth were extremely taken with. My father's sister, Aunt Amineh, a teacher and school principal, was active in the fight against illiteracy and started the country's first interscholastic children's magazine. Among our cousins, one of my Aunt Ester's five boys was a great horseman, an adventurer not at all interested in school; at eighteen he disappeared for days into the plains of Akkar and lived among the Bedouins. His sister, age sixteen, played the organ at church and was content to sit at the piano, immersed in Mozart's sonatas.

In Tripoli, as we walked in the narrow souks, the scent of olive soap filled our nostrils. In the distance the old Crusaders' castle overlooked the town. It was here, we were told, that the Crusaders learned the use of soap. We were also told how to identify descent from the Crusaders based on family name, and if not by name then by complexion and hair color. Down by the harbor, once a haven for sailing vessels from the world of antiquity, fishermen waited miserably in vain for a catch. A few old boats in the bay and one or two steamers beyond were the only signs of life. It would be many years, and Father would be dead, before this port was again transformed, into a refining center for oil from the wells of Iraq.

V

∼

I T WAS FROM THE FLOW of visitors and conversation in my
parents' house that I first learned of the emancipation of
women. An amateur writer called Beyhum was a particularly
vigorous defender. He had discarded his uneducated wife and
married a brilliant young Damascene, Nazik, who was charming
and cultured. She headed the first ambulance unit during Syria's
war against the French and remained active in public affairs.
Beyhum considered her the model of the new woman (and her
sincerity and tact helped her retain cordial relations with the former wife). In our Beirut neighborhood Julia Dimechkie, the second wife of a local notable, led a social reform movement. She
edited the first women's magazine in Lebanon and was energetic
in her demands for emancipation. Being one of the few Christian ladies to marry a Muslim, she attracted the attention of both
communities. As a practical matter, given his belief in the equality of the sexes, Father encouraged the first lady dentist of Beirut
to attend to us. She was an attractive European Jew who had a
growing clientele among veiled Muslim women.

I learned of the Bahai faith as well from one of my father's
visitors, a gentleman named Afnan, whose great-grandfather

had founded the faith. The creed appealed to Lebanese intellectuals and professionals, most prominently the country's first lady doctor. As a child, Afnan had lived in Iran; as a youth in Palestine. He had an exotic demeanor and spoke Arabic with a wonderfully charged accent. He and Father would sit for hours reviewing the issues of the day. In time, many more Bahais, mostly from Haifa, came to settle in Lebanon as perpetual troubles made them ill at ease in Palestine.

The summers, which for the most part we spent in Souk el-Gharb, a little village fronting the sea, brought an even wider set of regular visitors. Among them were a lady doctor from Cairo, an army engineer from Sudan, a Jewish dentist from Alexandria, a school principal from Haifa, and a prosperous Jewish merchant from Baghdad named Sassoun, who came every summer until the 1940s. Uncle Dumit had a grand residence nearby named Ghamdan, after the Arabian Palace of Sana, where notable Arab writers and poets gathered. Day by day we children watched them climb the stairs to his shady balcony and listened to the delightful play of their voices. The most distinguished of them came from Cairo. Ahmed Shawki, a dignified middle-aged gentleman called the Prince of Poets, was the most illustrious. May Ziadeh, an attractive young woman who radiated vitality, struck the gay note of the company. Born in Nazareth, raised in Lebanon, and living in Cairo, she was the most eminent female writer of her time. Her prose read like poetry, and her reflections on life sparkled with hope. My young uncle Anis was among her admirers, and thanks to him, as a girl I was able to shake her hand.

With each summer the Ghamdan circle of friends seemed to enlarge. Philip Hitti, a young Lebanese furthering his studies at Columbia University, knew more about Arab history than any of our family friends and fascinated us with stories about Arab

Spain, with pictures of the Alhambra Castle in Granada and the Great Mosque in Cordova. He told us of Arab mariners and travelers who had helped Columbus expand his knowledge of the earth. While Uncle Anis could enchant us with the rhythmic lyrics of the Moorish poets, Hitti was haunted by old glories of Cordova. In the prime of our inquisitive adolescence, we regarded Hitti as a heroic figure for his breadth of knowledge and gentle way. He wrote an inscription in my autograph book:

> The world is supported by four things only: The learning of the wise, the justice of the great, the prayers of the righteous, and the valor of the brave.

In the summer of 1924 there was much talk about the "unity of the Nile" among the Ghamdan circle. The expression was quite attractive to me at the age of fourteen, but more enthralling was the discussion about it that took place between Uncle Dumit and my father. My sister or I would often read the morning paper to them while they sipped their coffee. Both Uncle Dumit and Father were fond of Saad Zaghlul, who had demanded independence for Egypt, was exiled by the British first in 1919 and then again in 1921, and was now prime minister as leader of the Wafd Party, the most powerful voice for Egyptian nationalism. "Mark my words," Uncle Dumit said, "now the British insist on the unity of the Nile because they want the Sudan under their control. Once Egypt gets its independence they will start all over again, insisting on the disunity of the Nile."[1]

That spring my parents had toured the Holy Land, and it seems—at least from my father's diary of the trip—that the Arabs were not greatly worried then about British betrayal or Zionism. The European Jewish community was expanding slowly, adding small numbers of hardworking people to the agricultural area, and Arab laborers got along well with the Europeans. Father's main objective in Palestine was to meet his students and their families and to visit various institutions.

By his account, life was relaxed, and the days brought satisfactions and small pleasures. National schools for boys and girls were springing up. There was a sense of making up for time lost during the war. There were night schools and village welfare centers. The presence of a European minority provided an incentive for education, commerce, and agriculture. There was not much industry anywhere in the Arab East, but in this respect Palestine seemed in many ways superior to Lebanon and Syria.

Russian missionaries had started a number of girls' national schools in the Arab world, and although by the 1920s the missionaries could no longer sustain their support, the schools in Jerusalem managed to survive on local help and were ultimately incorporated within the Eastern Orthodox community. Wealthier Palestinians could attend British or French schools. Father seemed interested in one in particular: the Friends School in Ramallah, a Quaker institution. It was a modest enterprise that honored local traditions and Arabic culture and language.

Father's record of this trip devotes considerable attention to Birzeit College, a family concern, then still in its infancy, run by a woman of great talent. Father regarded Birzeit, its quaint green campus situated on a Jerusalem slope, as an expression of national determination and self-confidence. Some day, he felt sure, the Palestinians would have a university there that would change the life of the whole community. Forty years later, when I made my last visit to Birzeit, his prediction had been more than realized, as the university was greatly expanded, a lighthouse of learning for the whole area.

Father also visited the Schneller Institute, the first professional school for the disabled in Palestine. It was founded by German Lutherans, who continued to provide material and spiritual support. One of my youngest Tripoli cousins, who became blind at the age of seven, was educated there and eventually earned his livelihood playing and teaching music.

The most important of Father's visits was to the Arab College in Jerusalem, a fairly new institution tucked into a hill. There is not so much written about the college—which was started in 1918 by the British Mandate as a boarding school for Arabs and became the highest institute of education for Palestinian men—as there is about its remarkable director, Ahmad Sameh al-Khalidi. Described as a tall, dignified man, Khalidi was deeply conscious of future generations and national identity. A great believer in Arab culture, he was compiling a library of old manuscripts. All subjects, from medicine to good manners, interested him. He had a special affection for the rural areas of his homeland—the abundance of the earth, the trees, flowers, and plants of Palestine. His work there ended when the Arab College fell under enemy occupation in 1948.

That was all an unimagined future, of course, in the spring of 1924. Despite presentiments, we regarded the Arab face of Palestine as a certainty. In those days, when photography was rare, Mother insisted on purchasing a few pictures of the area— one of Lake Tiberius and its beautiful surroundings, the other of the Mount of Olives. These were framed and adorned our living room walls. Through them, we children traveled to the Holy Land in fancy, the image of the placid lake of Galilee arousing in me a kaleidoscope of dreams.

VI

~

THERE WAS A MISSION SCHOOL for girls in Beirut, which was founded in 1834 and boasted of being the first school for girls in the Ottoman Empire. My sisters went there when it reopened after the war, but Father had other plans for my schooling. In 1916 Marie Kassab, a fine Lebanese woman, had founded the Ahliah National School for Girls, the first such institution in the country. It had started with only sixteen pupils, was directed entirely by Arabs, and depended on Arab funds. Immediately after the war the student body grew to 250.

Some boys were allowed in the lower grades but not many. In any case, we girls didn't have much to do with them. My morning walk to school usually began with calling on my closest friend, Albertine, who had been born in Brazil. Next to Albertine lived Iffat, the daughter of a well-known Druze physician whose ancestors were the governors of a district in southern Lebanon. Veiled Nabiha, from a notable Muslim family, joined us next. She had the vitality of ten of us and wrote fierce essays attacking the French. Mary, who had come with her family from Jerusalem to Beirut when her brother was ready for university, spoke English better than any of us. Blonde Fauma had come from Damascus with her mother and two brothers after her father migrated to British Columbia in search of work.

In almost all weather we walked together through the narrow streets to the center of town, where the school was located. There were few cars in Beirut then, though mules, camels, and donkeys were a familiar sight in Ras-Beirut. We avoided the lonely and hazardous road through Hamra, a fashionable section now but then a field encircled by dunes of red sand, and walked the street known today as Clemenceau. Girls from well-to-do families came in horse-drawn carriages. The nicest were the beautiful Azm girls from Damascus, who didn't wear veils but covered their heads with scarves. The eldest was a talented essayist who wrote in French under the pseudonym Vie. Her dreams of becoming a well-known writer were shattered at the age of twenty, when her family arranged her marriage. Then there were sophisticated girls from the nouveaux riches families of Beirut and Damascus, who were interested only in French fashions and social events. When French schools later opened, most of those girls moved on.

Unintentionally, no doubt, the makeup of the school reflected the world's political tides. In the early 1920s a group of Turkish refugees, remnants of the Ottoman royal family, settled in Beirut, and five of their children came to our school. The lovely girls eventually found wealthy husbands in Damascus and Beirut. A number of White Russians, cultured people for the most part, had immigrated to our town. Like many refugees, they carried their grievances with them, but they also introduced some dash into our rigid social pattern; invariably, music and dance teachers were Russian. In the mid-1920s we had several European Jews at school. Aviva was thirteen when her parents came from Germany. She was gentle and loved the harmonica. I often visited her to borrow books and pictures. Whenever I went to see her she invited me to contribute a piaster to the "Jewish Home." What was this home? I hardly knew. A piaster was a lot of money to me then, but I could not refuse her.

The school was a two-story building with eight classrooms and an assembly hall. The compound was comparatively large. An immense fig tree dominated our playground. Folk songs and dancing were a vital part of school festivities, and the fig tree afforded excellent demarcation of stage center. When Western sports and Scouting became more important, the tree was felled to provide more space for organized parades.

In a small portion of the school's garden we were allowed to plant flowers and shrubs. We were also encouraged to gather samples of wildflowers from all over the country. With the help of friends, I collected a hundred specimens. I arranged them in a booklet, identifying them and the areas they had come from. But what names to use: Syria? Lebanon? Palestine? The boundaries of the Middle East seemed to be changing constantly in 1925. Even nature was victim to artificial frontiers.

One sunny afternoon in March of 1925, Father came home with an unaccustomed frown. Lord Arthur Balfour, he learned, would be stopping in Beirut on his way from Damascus and Jerusalem. The French were concerned about his visit and had taken strict security measures. Balfour had many enemies in the Arab world because of the infamous Balfour Declaration of 1917, in which he promised to give Palestine, which was neither his nor his government's to give, to the Zionists.[1] Father said that it was impossible for the million Arabs living in Palestine to understand why they should leave their home, the country of their ancestors, to strangers who claimed that it had belonged to them 3,000 years before. Their situation was comparable to that of the Turks vis-à-vis the Greeks, to whom the British had promised compensation if they took Smyrna and Constantinople. "How unfortunate," Father said, "that we do not have an Ataturk to frighten the West."

Balfour's promise disturbed me deeply. I took paper and pen and went to a quiet corner of the university chapel and began to write a letter to the king of England, imploring him not to allow the Zionists to take possession of the Holy Land. "Palestine is too sacred a country to give to the people who rejected the Master's message," I wrote. I was fifteen years old then. After citing all the historical evidence within my knowledge, I mailed the letter and returned home happily, with the feeling that the king would surely read it.

That evening Father sat with Uncle Dumit reading the Damascus newspaper accounts of Balfour's visit. I listened attentively. When Balfour arrived in Jerusalem from Haifa, the city was on strike. Black flags hung from houses and public buildings, and he was barred from the holy sites. When he inaugurated the Hebrew University, he said little and was heavily guarded. In Damascus it was worse; the city was in turmoil, and there were rumors of assassination. Balfour was rushed to Beirut in a darkened car and taken directly to his ship. He did not make any appearances.

For many nights after this, Father and his friends discussed the question of Palestine. I listened from my bedroom. During the day I searched for references in Father's books. I found a worn-out map labeled "Syria," which included Lebanon and Palestine. Were we not taught in geography class that Palestine was the southern part of Syria? Shouldn't the region be united under an Arab king? My imagination was daily inflamed by the hot arguments among my father and his colleagues. Father still believed that Britain would help Lebanon attain independence. Most of his colleagues strongly disagreed. "Who encouraged the Zionists to build a national home?" they demanded.

"No one loves us for our black eyes," goes a saying that Father often repeated. "These big nations are selfish; their major aim is to use us as tools to further their interests and ambitions. Now they want to impose the Jews upon us because they don't want them in Europe anymore." He had long maintained that "no one can give us independence; we must depend on ourselves," but, ever optimistic, he looked for silver linings in great-power rivalry.

Balfour's visit to Beirut brought to a head the people's frustrations with French rule. Just after his departure, news came that Syria was in revolt. The Syrians opposed the French policy of dividing the country into small districts, hampering the flow of people and trade in an area that had never been boundary-conscious. Waves of people had always traversed its major routes in pursuit of a livelihood. Tribes had always moved from place to place, following streams and the growth of vegetation. The Druze of southern Syria were especially affected by French constraints on their lifestyle, and their princes declared war. The French subdued the Syrians by bombing their cities.

Many families left Syria and settled in Lebanon. The troubles in Syria, in turn, created anxiety in Lebanon. Many politically liberal individuals departed for Egypt, where criticism of the French was welcomed. Criticism of the British was not.

At school, activities that nourished our patriotic feeling antagonized the French. Our principal, Marie Kassab, imparted to us a great deal of her dynamism and pride in language and tradition. Her right-hand helper was a severe disciplinarian who introduced us to Scouting. Miss Alice Abcarius was a contrast in appearance to Miss Kassab: her hair was short, and she wore manly suits or uniforms. Her manner was abrupt, whereas Miss Kassab's was gentle. Under Miss Abcarius's guidance, the Scouting movement gained popularity. In no time we were giving public performances and parading with our colorful uniforms, emblems, and badges through the streets of the capital. We went camping in neighboring villages and learned to love the warmth and beauty of our land.

This disturbed the French. They labored under the delusion that the Lebanese were more interested in European traditions and that it was easy for us to be assimilated into French culture. That culture intruded in subtle ways. In the spring of each year our school had a flower show. This could have been pastoral, but owing to French influence, it became a beauty contest. Twelve girls were chosen to represent twelve flowers. They looked lovely, but unhealthy competition sprang up among them. This was probably the first attempt at a beauty contest in Lebanon.

One morning in 1925 our principal addressed us during assembly in a shocked voice saying, "Orders have been issued to close down the school." She asked us to go home and await further instructions. Miss Abcarius stood up and insisted that all of the Scouts come to the school garden the next morning in full uniform. Nearly one hundred uniformed girls and boys showed up, arranging ourselves in rows to march to the government house. Our leader and the principal, both in uniform, led the way.

The whistle kept us in step as we marched along the crammed streets. A new high commissioner had been named, and people had come out to await his arrival. As we stepped into the Serail, or government house, we followed the crowd until we were admitted into the new commissioner's presence. We saluted and listened as our leader pleaded for the reconsideration of an unjust order. The high commissioner gave us his attention but no commitments. The local press, which had been outspoken in its criticism of his predecessor, was urging reform. As ours was a cause of great interest to the public, the school was reopened. But we had to give up our Scouting movement, double our hours of French language instruction, and refrain from public performance.

All of this was enough to blow up the bridges between us and the French. Although we studied more of their language and culture, we were more mindful of the chasm between us. The French suspected any form of education that awakened our self-respect. Even our school compositions were monitored. One day in English class we were asked to write on the following subject: "What country would you like to visit and why?" Two girls chose Egypt; Palestine figured more prominently than any country; then came India, Italy, and the United States. No one wanted to go to France. After that, new restrictions were imposed on the school.

Despite these tensions, we studied in a comparatively liberal atmosphere in which we could continue to express our patriotic feelings. As a sizable majority of the student body belonged to influential upper-middle-class families, the French authorities were careful not to antagonize them too much. Sometimes we felt the reins tighten, as when the school attempted to give equal emphasis to the study of French and English. Pressure from the French authorities corrected that.

VII

～

IN THE SPRING OF 1927, my final year at school, I was among fifty students aboard two red buses that carried us to Palestine. On the way south along the coast, we stopped briefly at Tyre. A road built over a sandbar now joins the ancient island to the mainland. It was in Tyre that Alexander had met matchless defiance. In revenge he destroyed one of the most glorious cities of all time. Painfully and relentlessly his army worked to construct a bridge to the island. Each night Tyrian divers swam underwater and tore apart the work of the day before. In the end the stronger force triumphed. The island was joined to the shore, and the city fell.

We drove from Tyre along a deserted coast to the high cliff that marked the frontier of Palestine. Cars were waiting on both sides of the border, but the British authorities quickly let us through. We were on the road to Acre, site of two important battles. It was here that the last garrison of Crusaders in the region was defeated, and here that 600 years later the Napoleonic fleet was repelled. Now the city was miserable with fear and anxiety. We pressed on. By the time we reached Haifa it was late in the afternoon. The harbor was being expanded, and the city's new quarter was crowded with apartments, built one behind the other, though Mount Carmel was not yet fully settled. From Haifa we crossed into the heart of Palestine, through prosperous villages and towns. We had been traveling since before dawn. When we finally neared the gates of Jerusalem, the stars were bright.

How to describe that first day in the Old City? Narrow lanes opened before us—a dream world of faces and objects; small shops with historical relics mingling with bread, dates, and fruit; windows displaying crosses of silver, ivory, or gold; piles of Damascene or Aleppine fabrics in all shades; carpets, blankets, and rugs of every pattern and hue; men, women, and children from the four corners of the world tight together in the ancient market and at the entrance of the Church of the Holy Sepulchre, the tomb of Christ.

Buried as it was amid heaps of gold and ornamentation, the tomb inspired no feeling of admiration within me. It was not until days later, while walking the quiet path of the Garden Tomb, that something spiritual within me was moved by Jerusalem. It happened again while visiting the Mosque of Omar, the Dome of the Rock, which stands in splendor over the timeless city. A sense of awe fell upon me at the sight of the dome, the Koranic quotations in gold, the rock in the center, the pious men sitting on Persian carpets or leaning against granite pillars. Something within me still thrills when I recall the atmosphere of tranquillity and meditation that permeated this mighty house of God. On one of our last evenings in Jerusalem, I felt that inspiring sensation again when we heard a Russian choir singing vespers as we headed to our hostel on the Mount of Olives.

During that Easter week the people of Jerusalem seemed at peace. Jews, Christians, and Muslims from everywhere were gathered in fellowship. To our young eyes, hatred did not seem to exist, nor fear, nor anguish, nor dismay. How little we knew.

The Arab face of Jerusalem was evident in the behavior, carriage, attire, and language of the city's dwellers. Arabic signs and slogans dominated the public centers and squares. Supplications and prayers in Arabic were heard from mosques and churches. Arabic had been the language for nearly 2,000 years of the history and the cultures of Jerusalem. It was as ubiquitous as the stones.

We left Jerusalem, visited Bethlehem and the countryside, and headed for the Galilee region, where we stopped at one of the Jewish kibbutzim. It was efficiently run. Nearly fifty babies had been left in the care of three women while the mothers labored in the fields and vineyards. There was a poultry farm, and for the first time we saw an incubator used to assist in the breeding of chickens. Herds of cattle were grazing. The colony, composed of Polish Jews who had recently settled in Palestine, was completely detached from the life of the area.

I found the Sea of Galilee inspiring. In the far distance, the mountains seemed like fortresses; by the shore the world was still but for a few fishermen drying their nets and the sound of the lapping waves. The Zionists were settling in these parts, beyond the reach of Arab interference. The British had given them lands that we were not allowed to visit. It took us Arabs a long time to discover that the kibbutz dwellers were not only tending chickens and farming the land but were also fabricating arms in hidden cellars beneath their quiet homes. In the Galilee region thousands of youths were being trained in methods of warfare. Arms were pouring into the land where Jesus had spoken of peace and love.

We returned to our buses and drove into the Huleh region. Mount Hermon was visible way off in the distance. Once, on a picnic near Huleh Lake, my father looked upon the same majestic peak and pointed out, "There beyond are the three sources of the Jordan. They rise from the feet of Mount Hermon: one into Lebanon, one into Syria, and the third into Palestine." Looking at it now I thought it was lucky the mountain was beyond the reach of man-made boundaries. No armies gathered at its summit with maps and rulers to partition it.

At the Lebanese border the French soldiers were annoyed when we woke them up. We certainly would have preferred to go right into our home without their sanction. "Christ and his disciples must have known this blessed region," I remember Father saying while on that earlier picnic. "How different it seems now with political frontiers carved into the heart of the land. The Romans united it all within their empire; the Arabs did the same a few centuries later, and after them the Ottomans. Why should history go backward when our world is getting smaller with the years?" Our buses crossed the checkpoint. Wheat fields stretched ahead of us. It was late when the faint lights of Sidon shone against the horizon. The coastal road carried us past the palm forest and brought us home to Beirut.

VIII

❧

SIXTEEN GIRLS GRADUATED with me in 1927. It is interesting to see how fate treated them.

The first to be engaged was the daughter of a banker. From three suitors she chose a rich young merchant from Jerusalem. A few months after the engagement, her father went bankrupt and her fiancé deserted her. Her dreams of marrying a charming prince vanished as she was unable to find another suitor. Beautiful, flirtatious Minerva married a Lebanese aviator living in Brazil. Iffat, who was always faster than the rest of us, married a cousin right out of high school and led an uneventful life. Mary went to England and married an Englishman. Intelligent Adeeba, the daughter of a university professor, whose good humor and angelic soprano voice made her the most popular in the class, chose to teach instead of going to the university (the children of professors were given free tuition). She stagnated, letting her many talents languish. Lucy, who had recently returned to Lebanon from Mexico, where her father had amassed a fortune, found herself in unkind circumstances. Her father lost his fortune gambling, and poor Lucy made an insecure marriage.

All of my other classmates married prominent men from Beirut or surrounding Arab countries. One died in an accident at sea during World War II. I was the only one privileged to go on to university.

I entered the American University of Beirut in the fall of 1927. My sister Selma and I were two of the university's twelve women students, among its first. Selma was a junior, and I was a sophomore. Co-education had been introduced at the university only in 1924, and women were not allowed to enter the freshman class. Most of them took their first year or two in a newly founded institution called the Junior College for Women (now the Lebanese American University). There were about a thousand men in the student body, and at times we twelve girls felt overwhelmed. Among the men, Egyptians, Sudanese, and Iraqis were joined by a few Ethiopians, Iranians, Greeks, and Cypriots, but most of the students came from Syria and Palestine. (At that time most Lebanese men attended the Jesuit University.) The boldest of our group of women was a married Egyptian lady, Ihsan, who was older than most of us. She came to class veiled, but this did not prevent her from leading many discussions or from encouraging the rest of us. Another, Edma, a Lebanese woman, was planning to be a doctor. A third, Nahil, was studying dentistry. Three European Jewish girls were studying medicine too.

Bayard Dodge, a remarkable, wealthy American, was university president then. He had been involved in relief work in Lebanon during the Great War and later married Mary Bliss, granddaughter of the university's founder. The Dodges, like the Blisses, were people of integrity. They subsidized large orphaned families and helped rescue young men from remote villages who came to them for education and counsel. Dodge was also a scholar with a genuine interest in the intellectual heritage of the Arab world. He learned our language and read a great deal of Arabic literature, even the more obscure texts. Mary Dodge, a woman of beauty and elegance, was always the first to visit mothers with newborn babies, the first to congratulate newlyweds, the first to convey condolences to the bereaved. All human events in and around the campus interested her.

The university offered no social life for the women students at that time. We had to be careful about our dress, careful about contact with the men around us, and we rarely attended social events. The only sport considered proper for us was roller-skating. We did, however, have ample opportunity for social work. The Brotherhood of Boys Service Club organized a night school for young workers. Our pupils were illiterate bootblacks, peddlers, and delivery boys. Before the age of ten, these boys had been thrown into the streets to beg or to work. Most chose work and did it honestly. For about two hours each evening we taught them the rudiments of reading, writing, and arithmetic. On the whole, they were easily disciplined, willing to sit through the cold nights of December and January on hard benches and in bleak surroundings to try to improve their status through study. Usually underfed, they wore thin rags and slept under staircases or in stables or shelters near churches or mosques. I can still hear them laughing at jokes or responding to orders with complete trust. They were optimistic despite the callous world around them and had a serenity beyond description.

The horde of illiterate boys was growing daily, though, and soon we had more than a hundred students and no room for all of the applicants. We expanded the curriculum, but remembering this now, I am struck that a half-century has elapsed since we took interest in fighting illiteracy and still it is one of the major problems of Lebanon and every Arab country. Many thousands of young boys still sleep under staircases or in shacks and are exploited daily. Fear and despair have taken deeper root, and a wave of rebellion is awakening their minds to revolt. The little done for them by voluntary aid has been only a drop in a great sea.

During my senior year the Brotherhood of Boys Service Club was reorganized as the Village Welfare Society to give remote villages medical assistance and simple literacy classes. The Village Welfare Society involved many college women, who took interest in the villagers' traditions and shared in a revival of folklore and music, crafts and arts. Life in those villages was often rough, but a fine fellowship was developed as we gained a sense of responsibility for our countrymen.

Although we were not allowed to attend the historical plays or variety shows that the college men put on regularly, women could participate in public speaking, and both the Arabic and English literary societies gave us opportunities to debate such issues as the emancipation of women, compulsory education, co-education, political freedom, and imperialism. Leading magazines, in particular *Al-Helal* of Cairo, sent prizes to the winners. Women were also able to attend lectures by prominent speakers whom the Arabic Department had invited, often to honor the anniversaries of great men. The most remarkable of these in my time celebrated the millennium of the poet Mutanabi. For this celebration poets came from Cairo, Baghdad, Damascus, and, of course, Beirut, for though Mutanabi is little known in the West, to the Arab student he is the most prominent of Arab-language poets.

Poetry was never the luxury of the few in the Arab world but rather a spontaneous medium of expression for all. As a famous Arab historian puts it, "The poet was the oracle of his tribe, her guide in peace and her champion in war. Everybody came to the poet for counsel." Mutanabi's verse exemplified the heroic traits of Arab poetry. He spent the major part of his life in the courts of Baghdad and Aleppo singing the virtues of the princes. Although the themes are commonplace, the lofty strains in his poetry have Homeric qualities.

On another memorable evening a German Orientalist discussed the thought of Al-Ghazali, the great eleventh-century mystic philosopher. Al-Ghazali, the son of a wool weaver in Baghdad, rose to eminence as one of the most incisive moralists of the Middle Ages. While in Baghdad, he recoiled from human vanities, adopted the ascetic life, and set himself on a hazardous pilgrimage to Mecca. After that he spent ten years in Damascus and then began traveling between Jerusalem, Damascus, and Baghdad.

Our knowledge of European culture came mostly through the writings and translations of modern Arab thinkers, primarily a group of provocative young authors living in Egypt. It was through the translations of the blind writer Taha Hussein and the editor Salameh Moussa that we became interested in Greek drama and philosophy. We found the works of Tolstoy and nineteenth-century Romantic writers especially captivating, but our acquaintance with Western thought was extremely limited. What we learned quite a lot about was the Orientalist fascination with archaeology. The historian and Egyptologist Dr. James Henry Breasted, then digging at Luxor under the auspices of the Rockefeller Foundation, lectured on the excavation of Tutankhamen's tomb. Breasted was eager to recruit young men from Lebanon, and his recurring visits, along with those of other Orientalists, had a great deal more resonance when my brother Elias joined the team at Luxor. Every spring upon his return, he brought us photographs of Ramses carved in the solid rock, Nefertiti, the colossi of Thebes, and the gold portraits and marvelous palace furniture of Tutankhamen.

Although free thought in Lebanon was constrained during the French Mandate, we had complete liberty to express ourselves on campus. On the second of November we commemorated the anniversary of the Balfour Declaration. We gathered in stormy public meetings, wearing black ribbons of mourning, and sent petitions and cables to people in authority and to patrons of Arab unity. Despite the desire of the French authorities to limit the sphere of the university's influence, it expanded. When we strove to fight ignorance and prejudice, or to run down corruption and greed, or to arouse public opinion to social injustice, the population was there to protect us. As senior university students in 1930 we supported the Egyptians' desire for a constitution rather than a titular monarchy and were angered by British opposition to it. We bitterly decried French efforts to impose the colonial language and culture upon Algeria.

Our alma mater, meanwhile, had no national stigma. We never felt we were in an American institution but rather in a great center of liberal ideas. While French schools hoisted the colonial flag over their buildings, the American University hoisted only a white emblem with the cedar tree. We never felt that the Americans pouring onto the campus had any claim over our minds. President Dodge initiated a beautiful tradition on the Prophet Muhammad's birthday intended to foster an appreciation of the spiritual values linking Christianity and Islam. It was in this world of vision and hope that we lived for four years, gaining faith in ourselves, pride in our heritage, and respect for the human ties that bind us to one another.

IX

W E WERE TAUGHT from early childhood to be proud of our mother tongue, but when I came to understand English I realized that our daily expressions can never be fully conveyed in translation. Our answer to "How are you?" for instance is "Fine, thank God," not "Fine, thank you."

Dependence on God was idiomatic in daily Arab conversation, not only in the rural areas but also in the city. If the weather was good, the common expression was "Thank God." If there was drought, it was "May it please God to send us rain." If the crops were poor, the people would ask, "Why is God against us?"

As we often summered in the mountains, we learned many phrases from our village neighbors. To a greeting of "Good morning," the reply might be "Another morning of light" or "A morning of jasmine" or "roses." We were taught specialized greetings. For masons and builders: "May God build with you." For farmers: "May God bless you with abundance." Upon entering a grocer's store: "God be with you." When we had paid for our purchases, the seller would reply, "May God recompense your giving." When a cloth merchant cut into a new piece of material for a buyer, he would say, "*Bil afia*," meaning "May you outwear it in health."

If a girl waited long to be married or had a luckless suitor, people would say, "Leave your gems in your jar till you get their worth." To an unmarried person: "May your turn for happiness come soon." To new parents: "*Mabruk*," meaning "May the child be blessed with the parents' love." To in-laws: "Your son is God's choice; your son-in-law is your choice." To the bereaved: "God has His painful justice. May He stand by your frailty." When we thought of renting a house in the mountains I remember Father saying to Mother, "The neighbor before the house, the companion before the road." When the house was full of guests, one heard the welcoming words "Narrow walls expand for friends."

As soon as we learned to enjoy reading, Father encouraged us to keep notebooks in which to record such proverbial sayings, not only those transmitted verbally but also those inscribed in wood and stone. Few were the vehicles of public transport, but most carried this verse: "Thou who ordaineth all movements keep us safe and sound." Few were the roadside fountains, but many had a motto exclaiming, "From the heart of the burning desert He giveth water to the thirsty." Few were the grand buildings in our town, but every one bore the words "All possessions belong to God. We are only passersby upon this earth."

A family trip to Damascus in 1929 underscored both parts of that last inscription. Our train chugged over the mountain ridges and into the Bekaa Valley, a patchwork of fields spreading from the banks of the Litani River and crisscrossed by irrigation canals. For centuries this had been the granary of Rome, feeding its armies. Animal drivers had carried its cereals to galleys waiting to cross the Mediterranean. Passersby, all of them. The train crept up the heights of the Anti-Lebanon Mountains and passed through rocky gorges between the cliffs. Damascus was near. A memorial honored the soldiers who had fallen in the Battle of Maisaloon against France in 1920, at the start of the French Mandate. Graceful poplars, willows, and oaks now lined the rails. Soon we were traveling alongside streams flowing to join the Barada, the largest of the seven rivers that water Damascus. At the entrance to the city Father asked us to visualize the waves of conquerors who had left their traces and to imagine St. Paul, who had had his conversion somewhere along this road.

"Now," Father said with pride, "we are in the oldest inhabited city in the world, the eternal abode of man."

After settling into the home of friends and sharing a delicious meal of stuffed lamb with rice, we made our first outing, to the covered Souk al-Hamidiya, the great market of Damascus, where braziers were shaping and engraving brass trays, lamps, and pipes; where carpenters were busy with hammers and chisels preparing their objects for mother-of-pearl inlays. All of these items, soon to be somebody's fleeting possessions, were embellished with proverbs in beautifully wrought Arabic script.

We walked on, and as we approached the immense gates of the Ommayad Mosque, Father indicated the intermingling of pagan, Christian, and Islamic architecture. The site was originally occupied by a temple to Jupiter. The columns had become part of the Church of St. John, which contains the head of John the Baptist and was built after the Roman Empire embraced Christianity. After Caliph Walid captured Damascus for Islam, in 635, it became a mosque honoring the Ommayad Dynasty, whose rule extended from India to the Atlantic. For many years Byzantine artists worked in the service of the caliph to beautify the mosque. Now hundreds of glittering lamps were flooding the sacred area with light, reflecting off the intricate mosaics.

Farther on, we came to a graceful white marble tomb in a dazzling mausoleum of multicolored marble mosaics, the resting place of Saladin. It had been restored, we were told, thanks to the German kaiser. Because of Saladin, the Crusaders never entered Damascus, and many ancient sites sat untroubled until recently, when the French army laid waste to them. On a picnic one day in the Ghoutah Valley, bees were humming over the bright flowerbeds in the morning sun and the younger children roamed about searching for the bridges that spanned the irrigation ditches while Father and eight of his former students sat sipping coffee and talking politics. These young men, sharply opposed to the French Mandate, described the ruin brought by French bombs. When we returned to our host's home, Father paused to recite the inscription carved over its door:

O thou who opens all doors;
O thou who knowest all knowledge.

I decided in Damascus to begin collecting from porticos, ceilings, votive fountains, mosques, and elsewhere the lines that had survived time, earthquakes, and the damages of war.

From the entrance of a small school in Damascus: "Search for knowledge even to the borders of China."

From the entrance to a prosperous farmer's house: "Search for riches in the bosom of the earth."

From the white marble frame of a garden basin: "Content your parents and thus content your God."

From the trim along a wooden ceiling: "Work for life as if you are living forever. And for afterlife as if you may die tomorrow."

From the door of a doctor's house: "Ask health for your
neighbor, and God bestows it upon you."

From the entrance to a trader's shop: "Make me grateful and
make men patient."

From the walls of a public library in Basra: "Shed light on my
heart, light on my tongue, light in my vision and light in
my soul," and "Labor for God as if you were facing Him."

At the main entrance of a university building in Aleppo:
"Honor your scholars; they are the heirs of your prophets."

At the entrance of the government house in Damascus:
"God's hand is with the united" and "God does not unite
His people in falsehood."

In one of the halls of justice: "Two things a governor needs:
justice that the strong may not take advantage of the
weak; generosity that the weak may not fear the strong."

On a ministry wall: "God does not bless a nation that does
not give justice to its people."

The older I grew the more I shared my father's belief that
Arabic is the loveliest language in the world. Throughout our
childhood he had missed no opportunity to encourage in us this
passion for the word. We used to play a game: Father would say
a verse and expect one of us to start the second using the last
letter of the rhyme. The player who could continue the longest
scored the most points. He was fond of chants and poems and
would hum verses to himself almost automatically, in a monotonous tone that had the effect of drilling these same verses into
our heads. Now, from time to time, I recall one of them:

The days unveil what is not known,
and messengers come with news untold;

Unknown the future and the past;
unknown to you the hidden scroll.

As a youth I didn't appreciate these verses as much I would as the years moved on. I savor them now. The lines he hummed when my brothers were quarrelsome:

Your brother, your brother, keep him close;
Unarmed through life a brotherless man.

The lines his old friend in Baghdad wrote while in financial distress:

I have known all the pleasures of life—
the dearest is well-being,
I have known all the bitterness of life—
the hardest is obligation to others,
I have carried iron and stone—
the heaviest is debt.

The lines he hummed so frequently they were like air:

We dwell in many homes on earth, the dearest is the place of
birth.

X

~

I HAD NOT EXPECTED my first job to be in Baghdad, but in 1930 graduates of Anglo-Saxon schools were unpopular in French-occupied Lebanon. For a respectable job, young women like me had to go to countries under British influence, which had long welcomed Lebanese graduates. My aunt, who was almost seventy and preparing to celebrate her fiftieth year of teaching, had been among the first Lebanese women to go to Egypt. But it was to Baghdad that my sister and I decided to go. The demand for teachers, physicians, and other professionals in Iraq was overwhelming. The British Mandate there was ending, and throngs of people were in motion. Assyrians, Chaldeans, and hordes of Kurds came to settle in Beirut and on the outskirts of our other cities, while young Lebanese traveled in the opposite direction.

We left Beirut late in September, and soon we were navigating the scorching Syrian desert. There was no marked road, only a lonely route, sometimes paralleled by a string of camels and interrupted by the occasional wonder. None was greater than Palmyra. Around sunset its sinister tower tombs came into view. The nobility had buried their dead here in layers, one on top of another. By the time we reached the ruined city it was dark. A full moon illuminated the broken colonnades that flanked deserted avenues and the forum. From about the sixth century BC, Palmyra had been the crossing point for the great trade routes: one from the Phoenician ports to the Persian Gulf, the other from Petra to southern Arabia. Eventually it became a Roman colony, with tariffs on luxuries from as far as India and China enriching the city and the imperial coffers. At its height, in the second and third centuries AD, this was the wealthiest of all caravan cities. Here Queen Zenobia had welcomed her guests, while hundreds of maidens festooned with flowers stood like living statues between the columns. Many of Palmyra's treasures have been snatched by European museums, but luckily these chiseled pillars could not be carried away.

Zenobia, a young Palmyrian princess, saw her husband assassinated while defending Roman territories. In a moment of pride she broke with Rome and endeavored to extend her own dominion. With an army said to have numbered 70,000, she occupied Egypt, established garrisons almost to Byzantium, and set herself on a throne that she believed Rome could not reach. In 274 the Emperor Aurelian came to put an end to her ambitions. Zenobia took flight on the swiftest of her camels; she was caught crossing the Euphrates and, when brought before Aurelian, insisted on clemency as a woman. She was bound with chains and carried off to Rome, where, wearing all her jewelry, she walked as a captive in the emperor's triumphal procession along with Goths, Amazon women, and vandals. Aurelian took Palmyra, but its people continued to revolt. Finally he destroyed the city and put its citizens to the sword. Zenobia made another life marrying a Roman noble and spent the rest of her days in a graceful villa on the Tiber.

In Zenobia's time it was a five-day camel journey from Palmyra to the Euphrates. Our American cars got us to the Syrian border town of Deir al-Zor on the river in several hours.

The desert between there and Mosul had many frontiers. At one time Mosul had been within Syrian territory, but France traded it to Britain in exchange for northern Syria; thus it became part of Iraq. From Mosul we took a short drive to the excavation area of Nineveh—then just a series of sandy mounds along the riverbanks, arid and desolate, marking the military seat of the Assyrian Empire.

The next day we headed for Baghdad via Kirkuk. As we drove, we saw strange little flames here and there in the desert, like Moses' burning bush but multiplied. Oil work was just beginning. Just past Samarra before sunset, we watched travelers descend from their camels, lay their mantles on the sand, and kneel for evening prayers. At twilight the gleaming minarets of the golden and blue mosques of Kassimain, a holy spot of the Shiites, signaled the approach to Baghdad.

As with most great cities, there is a legend behind the founding of Baghdad. It is said that the Caliph Al Mansur of the Abbasid Dynasty journeyed several times to the banks of the Tigris and Euphrates in the eighth century to find a site for the capital of his empire. He finally selected a village on the Tigris where a Christian monastery stood and named it Baghdad, meaning "Gift of God." That is the Arabic legend, but the name Baghdadu, for the Babylonian city dating to 2000 BC, appears in ancient texts.

The wall of the caliph's city had four gates: one leading to Syria, another to Basra, the third to Kufa, and the fourth to Persia. Nothing remains of those except the Arch of Clesiphon, which stands in the desert outside the city. From the ninth to the twelfth century, Baghdad was a city with no peer in the world, a center for scholars and mystics, abundant with the enticements of wealth and the spiritualism of poets, men like the Sufi Al-Ghazali and Abu al-Ala al-Maari. Its university preserved the works of Aristotle and Plato, and ancient manuscripts of India and Persia. No city of the Arab world, including Cordova, which equaled it in science and the arts, exceeded Baghdad in commerce and wealth. It was the unrivaled religious capital of Islam and the political capital of much of it.

My sister and I shared a house that, like all Baghdad dwellings, was entered through a small door that opened onto a courtyard. In the central garden stood an orange tree and a palm, with a few rose bushes and a dripping fountain. On hot days we retreated to an underground cellar. On autumn and spring nights we set up our beds on the roof, protected from the neighbors' curiosity by a wall. Each morning a boatman in a round *balam* rowed us across the Tigris. The tall palms with dangling red dates and the gardens and palaces along the riverbank gave an enchanting effect to our crossing. I did not have eyes enough to see all the haunting sights of this magical city. A horse carriage took us across Al-Rashid Street—named for Harun al-Rashid, who had reigned in Baghdad's greatest period—to the edge of the old city, and from there we walked the narrow alleys to our school.

It was the largest girls' school in Baghdad. King Faisal was deeply interested in women's education and vocational training, and he vigorously built schools and made land available to committees or individuals interested in opening them. (The same was true for hospitals.) Our job was to train young women to become teachers. All of the instruction, except for classes in English, was done in Arabic. We also introduced the girls to the joys of choral music, using patriotic tunes that struck a deep root in their heart. We taught them some of our Lebanese melodies as well and composed a school anthem. We took them for basketball games—their chief sport, which they once played in the palace garden with the princesses and their friends—and on historical excursions. The girls seemed eager to learn, and some took great interest in their developing country. One of our students, a talented girl named Sirriyah, became the first Iraqi woman to hold a diplomatic post. But many married early, limiting the scope of their activities.

I realized that I brought a very particular set of assumptions to Baghdad as a result of my own schooling. In the spring, as the city was making plans to welcome the first team of Arab aviators, the alumni association of my alma mater in Beirut decided to join in the celebration by holding a reception. I was chosen to greet the pilots in the name of Arab women, and I prepared a fiery speech expressing pride at seeing the first Arab aviators fly in Arab skies. I must have been strongly moved, for the speech disturbed the British authorities. I was reminded that Iraq was still under the wings of the British and that I had no right to display such emotions. This disturbed me a great deal. It became clear that Faisal and his team of dedicated nationalists would not be enough to loosen the hand of the British.

Taking care not to commit further political blunders, I concentrated on schoolwork and made a point of conversing with the many people we met. The *balam* man, the brick masons, the peddler who sold drinks to the thankless passersby—thousands of people like them were free from hatred in a city where there was a tremendous gap between rich and poor. Centuries of oppression had benumbed these city dwellers and blinded them to a better future. No one seemed to worry about the human gulf that widened with the passage of time.

Class discrepancies were sharper in the port city of Basra, and the effects of British dominance were unavoidable. On the first day of our holiday there, my sister, a friend, and I took a small boat to the point where the Tigris and the Euphrates meet, in the town of Querna, thick with palms and gardens.

"This is the site of ancient paradise," our oarsman cried. "Here is the hand of Adam." Here too, though he did not add, was a garrison of the British Army Corps.

Basra has been called the Venice of the East, with its bridges and ancient houses clustering along the riverbanks. In the curving streets, the Sabian silversmiths practiced their art, employing the same designs that their predecessors used hundreds of years ago. In the palace of an old Basra family, a precious collection of manuscripts awaited energy and talent to bring it to light. The streets disclosed the ancient headquarters of the Brethren of Serenity, an association of freethinkers. Here Sufism gave the world some of its noblest mystics, including the poetess Rabia, who, with her followers, relinquished the vanities of the world.

We walked through palm rows in the gardens of a Basra palace, marveling. Iraqi palms, an expert told us, numbered twenty million, and some reached heights of a hundred feet. Our guide indicated a palm that had borne fruit for at least two centuries. "Dates in Basra are not only the daily meal of the poor but they grace the tables of royalty," he said. "Their stones are fed to the cattle, and the trunks are used for bridges or boats."

He was speaking of old Basra, but the new one was quickly overtaking it. The port from which Sinbad the Sailor embarked to roam the open sea was populated with British dredges. One of them carried us to the oil fields of Abadan. The British captain boasted of his people's works. There were two Abadans: one modern, with gardens and charming villas, where the masters lived; another shabby, crowded and treeless, where the workers lived. These miserable people built those villas and planted the gardens and orchards but had no means to improve their own homes. And yet laborers by the thousands flocked to the area, coming from Iran, India, and Arabia. They barely survived on their low wages.

Oil was flowing out of Iraq. Western machinery had discovered it, and Western machinery was pumping it out and carrying it away. Abadan was then twenty years old. Over such a period a happier relationship could have existed between the master and the laborer. As the British captain piloted us back to Basra, some Scouts in our company argued with him about the right of the British to exploit their riches. He laughed at their naïveté: "We have found the oil and have every right to use it as we please." A gentleman in our company was angered by the British imperialists' habit of carving rich morsels of Arabia into separate entities to exploit. "Look there," he said. "Kuwait now seems an island encircled with neutral zones; it was once an integral part of Iraq. This wealthy area is ours no more."

"Don't you worry," one of the Scouts replied. "Some day we will restore it all."

The British had made a treaty conceding a small measure of independence to Iraq. Faisal was on the throne, and the country was accepted as a member in the League of Nations. This did not appease the ardent youth. British military bases were beyond the reach of local authorities. British planes hovered in their skies, and British men could march through their streets like victors. A feeling of uneasiness came over me as we left Iraq in June of 1931. Here was one of the richest countries of the Arab world. Now that oil was coming out of its bosom, its worth was becoming greater. Surely the West would not leave it in peace. The promises to its tired king were of no value. Faisal's health was failing as he left for Switzerland for more negotiations with the West. Soon news came of his death in Geneva. His son Ghazi, young and inexperienced, would be no match for the shrewd politicians of the West.

XI

❧

August 1931. The heat hung heavy over Beirut as an American Export liner, the *Exeter*, waited to carry us to the New World. The one-class ship had a heterogeneous collection of passengers. From Beirut, a number of businessmen were on their way to Italy; from Haifa, a few Polish and German Jews were joining their families in the States. My cabinmate was a sixty-year-old German Jew who was leaving her younger son behind and joining her eldest. The authorities in Palestine, she said, issued permits only to old people, ensuring that the younger generation remained to build their new nation. I was at the start of a journey that would take me to the University of Michigan at Ann Arbor for an advanced degree. The Old World accompanied me.

When we stopped in Alexandria for a day, a group of American youngsters gathered around me and listened as I told the old tales:

"Alexander lay on a couch in his tent when a gray-haired man appeared before him saying, 'An island lies where the loud billows roar, not far from the Nile.' When Alexander awoke, he ordered his men, 'Row me down the Nile.' At the island, near the mouth of the river, he declared, 'Here I will build a city that my name may be remembered for all time.'

"He called for sacks of barley and ordered his men to draw the outlines of his city by dropping the grains on the ground. Suddenly it was as if a large black cloud arose from the Nile, as a hundred birds swooped down and devoured the grain. A wizened fellow standing nearby exclaimed, 'Men from all over the world will flock to this city to be fed; it will be prosperous and great.' When Alexander died, he was buried in Alexandria in a gold coffin. A few years later, to pay his mercenaries, one of his generals melted the gold, and the remains of Alexander have long been lost."

Our ship left port. On the seventh day, it neared the Straits of Gibraltar. The British flag swayed in the midday breeze off the great rock. To the ancient Greeks, this was the limit of the known world. To the Arabs, it was the beginning of a new one. The daring Arab leader Tarik, who gave the rock his name ("Gibraltar" comes from "Jabal Tarik," meaning "Tarik's mountain"), led his armies to the land saying, "The sea is behind you; the enemy is ahead. Choose glory or shame." In Spain the Arabs built an empire that lasted nearly eight hundred years. They built Cordova, encasing its mosques and palaces in jasper and marble. Learned men hastened to its libraries. Its university courtyards welcomed the great philosophers Avecinna, Avempace, and Averroes. From every corner of the continent scholars gathered for inquiry in the disciplines of medicine, mathematics, and astronomy. In the rural valleys the Arabs introduced peaches, apricots, pomegranates, figs, and dates, and in the villages they brought the lyrics and melodies of the Orient, which troubadours carried into the heart of Europe.

A small group of students were crossing the ocean with me. There was a medical student from Italy joining a Rockefeller

Research Center, a Swede planning to work in the States, a Belgian chemist intent on furthering his education, and an American Rhodes Scholar returning home.

Although America and the world were in a depression, benevolent organizations were providing financial help to students. I was headed to Michigan as a Barbour Scholar, one of thirty women to receive a grant from the fund set up by an illustrious alumnus to promote the spread of women's education in Asia. I was joined at the university by young women from China, India, Korea, Burma, Japan, and Turkey.

As the ship approached the U.S. shore, the towers of New York cut against a gloomy sky. I saw the Statue of Liberty and, like many a newcomer, was inspired by its symbolism. A lady volunteered to write the inscription from its pedestal in my notebook: "Give me your tired, your poor, your huddled masses yearning to breathe free, the wretched refuse of your teeming shore. Send these, the homeless, tempest-tost to me. I lift my lamp beside the golden door!"

I spent a delightful week in New York visiting the sights and meeting members of the Arab community. Among the talented young people, the talk was all of Khalil Gibran and *The Prophet*; of Gibran's contemporary Elia Abu Madi, whose "Land of Stars," set to music and rendered by the soprano Ferouz, evoked the inspiring evenings of his native village; and of the loss of Fawzi Malouf, whose poem "On an Air Carpet" expressed the longings of man for something beyond materialism. Malouf had died in Brazil in the prime of youth and, like Gibran, became an idol of the younger generation. And yet the youth were also being lured by life in the New World. Unaware of the changing life in the East, they were unlikely to return.

It was different at Michigan. The Arab student group there was comparatively small—two Iraqis, two Lebanese, one Syr-

ian, six Palestinians—and our nation's future tended to be a
matter of passionate, personal concern. Whenever we met, it
was natural that we spoke about Palestine, the most acute problem in the Arab world. Most of the Jewish Americans we knew
seemed uninterested in Zionism as a political movement. Some
had come from Europe many years before, and in no way were
they ready to give up their privileged position to go to the Middle East. An American friend arranged for us to meet the
Kahns, a wealthy Jewish family who lived in a suburb of Detroit. Their garden and lovely furnishings spoke of settled prosperity. Mrs. Kahn was gracious and outspoken. In her opinion
the Jews were happy in America and must never think of leaving. She found the idea of a national home repellent. She shared
the American Council of Judaism's position that "Judaism is a
religion and not a nationality." Such encounters gave me an ease
of mind. I thought that the Balfour Declaration would never
find a hearing in the States.

My Palestinian friends were skeptical about both my political conclusions and my opinion of America as a vale of happiness. A young lawyer insisted that I give myself time to discover
the truth. I got a sense of that when an attractive Catholic girl
in the dorm was reprimanded by her comrades for dating a Jewish boy and took refuge in my sympathy. As I observed more, I
came to conclude that the Arab East knew a type of tolerance
rarely found elsewhere. Black students, I noticed, made up only
a small minority at the university, and they were quite aloof.
When it was my privilege to have contact with some of them,
they unloaded their painful recollections. It seemed to me then
that it would take a long time to change the situation. University circles seemed to appreciate the stirring Negro spirituals,
and at their religious gatherings I was impressed by the voice of
the preacher, for whom faith was a living reality. These people

visualized the Holy Land with a freshness and clarity, though not one of them had ever been to the East.

As I became more intimate with my new environment, I took special interest in the musical life of the country and in the significant share that colored people had in it. Jazz struck me as being exciting and challenging. I bought a secondhand radio through which I was able to enjoy inspiring concerts and plays, grand operas and orchestral ensembles, choral recitals and popular songs. A new world of beauty unfolded in my small apartment on South University Street. Time and again as I recall the past, I am moved by the way some of the popular songs expressed the human condition of American life. "Brother, Can You Spare a Dime?" was the lament of an unemployed citizen who told of what he had done for his country and how he had been thrown aside in the Depression.

Living in the quiet university town of Ann Arbor, we rarely noticed the destitution that stalked the great cities. The ugly picture of unemployment that I saw in the parks of New York was again evident in Detroit and Chicago. Though we were mostly sheltered from it, Michigan was in crisis. The banks were closed and the atmosphere was uneasy. Some young Americans vented their indignation against the nation's leaders. They dreamed of an era of equal rights and privileges. Because of the economic crisis, bright youth had to abandon their education. University graduates had to accept unskilled jobs. Insecurity reigned. Indeed, it was strange to learn of this and continue to enjoy the benevolence of wealthy Americans toward foreign students.

It was strange, too, to tour Michigan's new prison, of which the state was greatly proud, and to realize that the unfortunate prisoners were in many ways more fortunate than the unemployed citizens who spent their nights outdoors on cold benches and went from day to day with empty stomachs. The minute we entered the compound, we were struck by the spacious sports fields and the provision for all kinds of gymnastics.

The several buildings, like floors of a hospital, were designated for the various types of penalty, as well as for recreation and work. Small industrial units for food products and canning were in operation. The large bakery had prisoners preparing bread, biscuits, and cakes. Inmates in other units made clothing and shoes. Many wore neat white trousers and white shirts. Those who were working wore navy blue uniforms. The sight was similar to that of laborers in any factory. The prison had a library where silence was observed. A printing press issued a weekly pamphlet and gave prisoners a chance to use their creative talent; an adult school allowed the inmates to improve their education. There were art classes in woodwork, textiles, crafts, weaving, and pottery. Few prisoners were in strict confinement; most were allowed to move from one unit to another. At one point we heard a middle-aged prisoner playing a Bach prelude on an organ. The sound was glorious, though there were few listeners.

I suppose what was most evident to me in Depression-era America was the respect of all classes of society toward labor, in all its forms and at all stages of life. Children between the ages of ten and fourteen woke before dawn to carry the morning papers or to lend a hand delivering milk or groceries. Some tended gardens, picked apples, mended furniture, or worked in laundries. At rush hour around school areas, children took over traffic duties from the police, allowing their comrades a secure crossing. Compulsory education seemed to reach every class of society. I realized that this abundance of energy was intimately linked with the desire to make money. Even the very young were trained to expect pay for whatever work they did. Children exacted money from aunts or neighbors and sometimes from parents for work that, back home, our children did freely. An array

of tasks that our children ordinarily did for joy would be done
only for pay in the States.

I often regretted that a certain grace in human relations had
disappeared from the social pattern of modern America. Perhaps in the rural areas it was different. In the cities, and even in
a place like Ann Arbor, the more I admired America's organization and discipline in public and private life, the more I understood why grace had vanished. Life was a swift race, and no one
could afford to loiter.

On campus, meanwhile, world events roiled debate. The poet
William Butler Yeats came to appeal for the cause of a free Ireland. Count Sforza came and denounced the Italian Fascists.
The Chinese students were disturbed by Japan's attack on
Manchuria, and the Koreans were troubled by Japanese aggression, while the Indians had an enviable serenity. Haridas
Muzumdar, a brilliant young Indian, had just published a book
titled *Gandhi Versus the Empire*. Although he spoke with vehe-
mence against British politics, his heart was free from contempt. The Gandhian ideas of nonviolence carried all his
hope—and not just his. When Tolstoy's daughter came to speak
at the university, she expressed veneration for Gandhi, telling of
the long correspondence that her father had with the Indian
leader. She spoke with understanding of the revolutionary
regime in her country, anticipating that Russians would experience a lengthy period of trial and error.

In meetings between Indian and Arab students, we shared
our anxieties and discovered how much we had in common.
Years later I would find something Nehru wrote from his prison
cell to his young daughter:

When the British declared that they are willing to establish a
National home for the Jews in Palestine, Palestine was not a

wilderness. There were Arabs and non-Arabs living there, Moslems and Christians. Palestine is essentially an Arab country and must remain so. The Arabs must not be crushed and suppressed in their homeland. Both Arabs and non-Arabs can cooperate together and build one progressive country. Zionism is a colonial movement. The generous offer of the British was made at the expense of the Arabs. It is certain that Arab Nationalism in Palestine will not be crushed.

The Arab students' meetings, like those of all the national groups at Michigan, began with anthems and songs. We often used a popular song by the young Palestinian poet Toukan titled "Mautini" ("My Homeland"). Once I thought it might be useful to write something in English that could engage the Asiatics as well as the few Europeans who joined us. The music was as simple as the words. Although I now find it banal and out of step with modern songs, I reproduce it here to emphasize that for Arabs the problem of Palestine was our common denominator, the core of our thoughts and aspirations:

O Palestine Sweet Palestine
My heart is kindled on thy shrine
thy shrine
They call you theirs
I call you mine
O my beloved Palestine.

After I had been in Michigan for a year, my eldest brother, Elias, decided to come to the Engineering School. My first concern was to find a better apartment for us to share. Some of my American friends advised me to wait; perhaps he would prefer to be on his own. This was an idea not at all familiar to me as an Arab. Family ties draw us together across time and age. We do not define independence as Americans do. When my brother came, we had a great deal to agree on and a great deal to differ about, but we were linked in daily contact and enjoyed the experience of university life. Now that I am the mother of four children, I see more clearly what intimate relationships Arab families have. Our children grow up encircled by an affection and attention that often seems beyond their need. This encircling compassion can be of great value when life goes amiss. Our old people are not left to live in solitude, and the young ones are not separated from their kin. On the whole, I think, youth in America live in loneliness.

XII

❧

AMERICA HAD SHOWN ME its promise and its contradictions. In the spring of 1933, I returned home, stopping in Europe on my way. Here are a few scenes of the Old World before the wars.

Manchester seemed to be all business. In the Arab communities Lebanese and Syrian émigrés were busy supplying African towns with new fabrics and opening markets for British products. Commerce was their main concern. The Houranis were an exception in that respect. My uncle Fadlo Hourani had come to this city nearly thirty years before, when he was in his early twenties. He too was a businessman, and quite soon his commercial enterprises expanded to the African coasts, mostly Kenya and Ghana, and as far off as Trinidad and other islands of the West Indies. At the same time, he lavished money on his native town in southern Lebanon, making roads, building a cemetery, and lending help to a private mental hospital and the country's public projects.

He dreamed of building a model school in his native town as soon as the Depression was over. Much of my holiday was spent in the company of his three daughters, one of whom was destined

to become my sister-in-law. The sons were Oxford scholars heading toward brilliant intellectual careers. Brought up in England's
conservative public school tradition, they spent hours among their
books and writings. The middle lad, Albert, hardly eighteen at
that time, had written a fine work on medieval cathedrals. He was
too shy to show it to me, so I looked at it secretly. His descriptions
were remarkably delicate, and helped me to see the Gothic monuments of England with new eyes.

Growing up in the Arab East, where I was frustrated by political
tides that ran counter to justice and integrity, I found the vision of
orderly, disciplined England both uplifting and alarming. In London the names of great men in Westminster Abbey, the statues of
the empire builders in Trafalgar Square and elsewhere, even the
open parks, proclaimed freedom. How often, as I passed near the
House of Commons, did I ask myself, "Why do its members impose their power on weak nations when they know so well that
justice is the aspiration of mankind everywhere?"

I made a point of spending several days among the ennobling
grandeur of Oxford, and from there I traveled to experience the
inaugural season of the new Shakespeare theater at Stratford-
on-Avon. On the train, I sat next to a plain-looking middle-aged
woman. We conversed about the weather and landscape, and
then she inquired whether I was French or Italian. When she
learned I was an Arab from Lebanon, her whole bearing
changed. There was no curiosity in her glances, only restraint. I
busied myself reading *Julius Caesar*, which I would see performed that evening, but a feeling of self-defense came over me.
Why should this person disdain me? She was not half as educated as I, she could not speak the languages I spoke, she had
had no chance to travel, and, on top of it all, both in attire and
appearance she was far inferior to me, if that counts at all in the

balance. I brooded on this for a while but soon found myself transported by the verdure of the countryside, thrilled by the cosmopolitan crowd that gathered at the theater and privileged to attend the performance. The audience drank in every syllable. It was like being in a state of worship in one of God's shrines. The play ended, and the spell of Roman glory evoked by Shakespeare's verse was broken by the monotonous, majestic strains of "God Save the King."

For one complete month Paris haunted me. At the Louvre, I searched not only for the Venus de Milo, the Winged Victory of Samothrace, and the Mona Lisa but more particularly for the treasures taken from Arab lands. I toured the Oriental wings, viewing relics from Palmyra, Babylon, Byblos, Damascus, Sidon, Tyre, Cairo, and Thebes with a mixture of happiness and dismay. An Italian companion reminded me that Italy too had lost some of its loveliest masterpieces. What does it matter, after all, I finally told myself, as long as they are within reach of humanity?

In the Bibliotheque Nationale hundreds of undeciphered Arabic manuscripts from Andalusia were heaped one on top of another awaiting translation. In one corner a German Arabist was studying Sufism. He had recently found many treasures on the subject in the Vatican library and was hoping to find more when he traveled to the Estorial in Madrid. From Leyden University a young man was gathering material on Al-Ghazali. Another young scholar, from the University of Rome, was poring over Arabic manuscripts on astronomy. A Danish girl was interested in books on the sources of *The Arabian Nights*. Once again this confused feeling stirred in me. How had this enormous heritage been so dispersed, and why had it been left in neglect for so long?

French culture was at its zenith in the 1930s, and its influence reached across the Mediterranean to Romania, Bulgaria, Turkey, and Iran. The Sorbonne area abounded with students from those places, as well as from Lebanon and Syria, wasting their time and their governments' money among the cafes and pretty women of the Latin Quarter. They had given themselves up completely to this bohemian atmosphere, where women of all types were within reach—and, with them, wine, gaiety, and forgetfulness.

Pictures of nudes exhibited by the dozen on side streets, daring books illustrating the poetry of Baudelaire and his followers, sensuous scenes in theaters, nightclubs, and movie halls—this throbbing world completely upset these students' values. Few young people were strong-willed enough to resist its seductions. As they attempted to rid themselves of their national identities, they stopped using their own languages and were even ashamed to confess their origin! Voltaire, Rousseau, Rabelais, Villon, Baudelaire, and Sartre drew them away from the East. Here was a generation frustrated, beguiled, completely lost to itself. I could not refrain from comparing them with the Arab youth in the United States, who took pride in their heritage and country, who at times, like the Indians and Chinese, wore their native costumes, who lost no opportunity to embellish colorless English with their own proverbial language.

The French youth were to me the most perplexing. With nothing of the determination or healthy dynamism of the Americans, they spoke with sarcasm and unrestrained cynicism. For all its beauty, Paris seemed cold. One day my wanderings brought me to the vicinity of a new mosque, the gift of Tunisians and Algerians. As I sat contemplating it, two Algerian young men sat beside me and immediately asked whether

Arabic was my native tongue. Indeed it was, I answered. They seemed to envy this privilege that they did not have.

Two days before I left Paris, a headline in an Arabic newspaper at a stand on the Seine caught me up. *Monopole* is the word I remember. Lebanon and Syria were seized by strikes as the French tried to monopolize tobacco, salt, sugar, and soap, the main products of our land. The economy of our country had to be regulated to serve the interests of the mandatory government. My thoughts went back to Gandhi, whose passive resistance gave faith to his people. "It is not easy to do the same in Lebanon and Syria," said my French companion Lucienne. "You have been accustomed to the snobbery of the West. Passive resistance means deprivation of comfort and ease. You have come to depend on us to give you these."

In Austria, I thought the charming town of Innsbruck—the colorful attire of its policemen, the happiness of its children—reflected a contented people. Instead of fashionable cars, they rode bicycles. Down from the Tyrol and into Salzburg, we found a town swarming with Alpinists on holiday. Then news arrived that Chancellor Dollfuss had been assassinated. Details were not known, but it was generally believed that the Nazis were the culprits. When we arrived in Vienna, faces were unsmiling. We followed the mourning crowds, Austrians from all over the country, on their way to pay last respects to their leader. It was a veneration that Dollfuss had not enjoyed in his lifetime. The cathedral choir sang from Mozart's *Requiem*; it still echoes in my memory, and with it the "Agnus Dei": *Dona nobis pacem*.

There was much to see in Vienna when the funeral was over: the Danube, the Ruegstrasse, the museums, the opera house, the University of Vienna. In the city's cafes and squares the melodies of Mozart, Beethoven, Schubert, and Strauss continued to play. One early morning my companion and I went to the garden tombs of Beethoven and Mozart. We were speaking French, and a poorly dressed old woman sitting on a bench knitting inquired whether we came from France. "No," I said quickly, "Lebanon," then added, "near Damascus, Jerusalem." Despite her frailty she jumped up and hugged me. "The Holy Land! How lucky you are. How I wished I could go there before I die. Now it is too late." Her hands reminded me of something out of Albrecht Dürer, or perhaps Rodin—suppliant, lifted in prayer in a darkening time.

Almost every shop in Budapest, it seemed, carried a certain postcard with a map of Hungary after the Great War. When the bottom of it was pressed back, the country's usurped provinces sprang again into sight. Like so many of the smaller European nations, Hungary had suffered, and one could feel the people's bitterness toward the Western powers that had stripped their country of its rich lands. Years later, in the midst of the war that could now only be sensed, I would meet a Hungarian musician, Frieda S., who sought refuge in Beirut. "My home," she joked mordantly, "was oddly situated at a new boundary. Half of it was in Hungary, and half of it outside. I had to have a passport every time I wanted to go to the bathroom!" When I saw it, Budapest had a veneer of gaiety. Viennese waltzes, played to the rhythm of American jazz, kept the morale a little above the level of despair.

The Italian ship on which we embarked for home at Trieste in 1934 was packed, mostly with young Jewish couples leaving Germany or Czechoslovakia for Palestine. Some had heard that Iraq needed experts and were ready to take a risk there; if things did not turn out well, they could easily go to Palestine. The British authorities required no formalities for their entry into the Arab East. It was difficult to guess whether there were undesirable people among them, people charged with crimes or defiance of law. No life history was required. The same would not have been true if these Jewish couples tried to enter England, France, America, or Canada.

I could not but be gentle with the young strangers. I told them how beautiful my country was but how few work opportunities there were for our educated youth, some of whom were trying their chances in Africa. The young strangers said it mattered little to them whether they settled in Africa or anywhere else. They had no sentimental attachment to Palestine, most of them having renounced religious belief. Many had no notion of a historic connection with the country. They were daring youth of Europe, virile, energetic, interested in sports. They loved art and felt an attachment to German culture. They knew little English and no Hebrew at all, just a few words of Yiddish, which they hesitated to speak. What an irony of fate this all seemed. These promising young Europeans rejected by Europe were trying to find a place in the East where they could live in peace.

Some commented on the heat aboard ship. It was August. I told them that it was nothing compared with the desert heat. The ship stopped in Larnaca, Cyprus, where peddlers brought delicious grapes on deck and heaps of lace fabrics for sale. The British-controlled island looked poor and miserable from the coast. Three Turkish girls ages ten to fourteen came on board. They were being sent to serve wealthy masters in Damascus. Enough money had been paid to their families to allow them an absence of several years, and possibly a marriage away from home. Through British leadership, Europe had changed its policy regarding slavery in the nineteenth century. Why, then, did the British close their eyes to it now, when it was being practiced on an island that they claimed to protect? Such protection was limited to stationing warriors and storing munitions.

Dockers in the port of Jaffa were unloading the luggage of the nearly one hundred Jewish passengers whose company I had shared from Trieste. The authorities who came to the port to receive them spared no effort to bestow warmth. A new town was being built for the immigrants near Jaffa. It would become Tel Aviv. Otherwise, the plan was to disperse the newcomers throughout the country. Once the passengers were ashore, I asked the captain whether we were ready to leave for Haifa. "Not yet, young lady," he said. "We still have a lot of freight." I had seen the luggage being unpacked, but now a crane was unloading scores of big cases as well.

"What is there in the cases?" I asked. The Italian captain smiled. "We are not saying," he said slyly.

His young assistant whispered in my ear: "Ammunition. Every ship comes loaded with ammunition. A great war is going to take place on these shores, I tell you," he said. "They cannot turn all the swords into plowshares. We cannot take care of the thousands of requests for passage for Jews. Many of them do not know much about it. They are seduced. They are misled."

"What is your name?" I asked.

"Moshe," he said. "I am also a Jew, from Milano. We are happy there, and my father is getting wealthy. I shall never leave Milano, even if I can dig gold in Tel Aviv."

When we reached Haifa at sunset, the steamer had the luggage of only eight passengers and practically no freight to unload. Haifa had always been a prosperous rival of my hometown. I had been in this harbor twice before, and had even been invited to teach in one of the city's new schools right after graduation. My parents did not want me to take the risk. Beneath the calm of Palestine was a smoldering fire.

It was morning when we arrived in Beirut. A hot breeze blew gently. The harbor had expanded since I had left, but work was still scarce. French ships monopolized business, leaving little for the Greek and Italian steamers that had kept this port busy for many centuries past. I hardly noticed, though, in the excitement of being home, restored to the affection of my family.

XIII

❦

IN THE FALL OF 1935, after one year in a deputy position, I
assumed a role that would be mine for the rest of my working
life, as principal of my alma mater, the Ahliah National School
for Girls. I was barely twenty-six years old, and I knew that,
amid so much uncertainty, my only chance lay in the success of
that first year.

The Ahliah National School was one of the few educational
centers that rubbed uncomfortably against the French authorities in Lebanon. Founded in 1916, it experienced its golden
years when I was a student, right after World War I. National
spirit and morale were high then. Lebanon had been promised
independence, and we could visualize it. Now, with France still
retaining its Mandate over us, it was a trying time for dreamers.
When I returned to the school as an administrator in 1934, the
day-school enrollment was barely 150, mostly Lebanese and
Syrian girls, and there were more than twenty-eight boarders,
mostly Palestinians, some of them boys. The classes ranged
from kindergarten to the last grade of high school. A year later
the number of boarders fell to eighteen and that of day students
to one hundred. Few of the girls were enthusiastic about their

education. To my dismay, I realized that the number of girls who went to college then was not much larger than it had been in my time. Moreover, the chances of finding a job in Lebanon or Syria were extremely small.

Our school was alien in an atmosphere permeated with French culture. In 1935, the public expected us to copy the French schools and to identify ourselves with their programs and systems. The French authorities in Lebanon wanted to embed a love for France in the children. Hundreds of French schools, especially those dominated by a powerful clergy, were striving toward that goal. There were fantasies of building up a Lebanon completely won over to the French mode.

Although I had a fairly good knowledge of the French language, and although I had recently visited France and enjoyed the cultural riches of Paris, at heart I was hungry for expressions of national identity. Like a stray bird returning to its own, I yearned to speak my language, to read Arabic books, and to foster Arab independence and solidarity. I hated to be addressed in French while in a shop. I felt ill at ease when old and new friends greeted me in French. How much of a compromise should I make to come to terms with my own people? That question preoccupied me, as I could see that bit by bit Lebanon was being detached from its Arab roots.

The academic program that I inherited, forced on the school by the French ministry, included French language and literature, some English, math and sciences, as well as history and geography. Instruction was to be in French. A lot of memory work was expected from the girls. Study of the history and geography of France was compulsory. Ahliah taught Arabic and attempted to teach the history of Lebanon and the Arab countries, but in the crowded schedule the latter was never done properly. There were also two recreation periods: gym and drawing. Sports were rarely practiced because of the small compound, but there was an effort to play basketball. The girls learned folk dancing for a spring show to which parents were invited. It was colorful and stylish, these affectations serving to conceal poor performance.

Thus, except for the slight addition of the Arabic language, the program was a copy of the French system. The girls were prepared for two government exams: one after six years of primary work, the second after four years of secondary work. French authorities expected the school to make an effort to see that French was spoken at recess. Students who insisted on speaking Arabic were to be singled out, and those who persisted were to be given detention.

To undermine Lebanese unity, the French Mandate was also emphasizing sectarianism. Nowhere were its effects more dangerous than in education. The authorities realized that they could not destroy the strong framework built by hundreds of Catholic missionaries across Syria and Lebanon, so they exploited it. They were not interested in religion or the system's ability to answer our needs; they were happy that the French language was gaining ground and putting Arabic in eclipse. Talented Lebanese used French as a medium for private and public expression. Theatrical groups from France dramatized Racine and Molière to the applause of enthusiastic audiences. French books and periodicals were sold by the thousands.

I was convinced that Western culture could be harmful if we did not adapt it to our lives through the medium of our language. My thoughts were not popular among the students' parents. Above all, they wanted their children to speak French fluently. One prominent politician who would play an important role in the country discovered that his daughters, after three years with us, did not speak fluent French, so he moved them to a foreign school. We had no allies, even among the Muslims, who sup-posedly professed greater allegiance to our Arab heritage.

So the school needed friends; my primary duty was to make them wherever they could be found. To search for the old friends was as important, if not more, than to make new ones. When I visited Bayard Dodge, then president of the American University, he was most encouraging. Always full of optimism, he gave me a sense of purpose in service. It little mattered then whether I was rowing with or against the ideological current. What was impor-tant was the caliber of service to the youth of my country. My father, now in retirement after forty years as a university profes-sor, never failed to remind me that nothing is more important than the human side of education. He wanted me to get to know my pupils and my teachers as intimately as I possibly could. That meant sharing their daily problems and living through their anxieties. To do that, I had to understand their family backgrounds, a project that I would always find stimulating.

My most serious internal problem that first year as principal was a French teacher who had been sent to us by the authorities. Madame C. was paid a salary four times higher than that of our best teachers but worked less than any of them. Her atti-tude in class was arrogant. She belittled our country and its tra-ditions and made the girls feel ashamed. Upon learning of this, I did not hesitate to request an interview with the French chan-cellor of education, who received me kindly and listened to my complaints. When the year was over he agreed to place the teacher elsewhere, but he also cut the subsidy allotted to us by the ministry. Many colleagues at the time blamed me for my im-patience; however, I felt at ease. The atmosphere of the school became better. I could face my girls every morning with a mes-sage of reassurance and love. Day by day, they regained confi-dence in themselves and pride in their heritage.

My sister Selma, who had been at the school for two years before my arrival, was an indispensable help to me. We were different but complementary characters. One of her greatest attributes was an even temper, and she tended to our boarders with a mother's care. During illness or epidemics, she kept a level head. As our school expanded to meet the pressing needs of Palestinian children, Selma and her partner, Mohiba, bestowed confidence to panicky mothers and calmed nervous children.

Our section of the city was not overbuilt then. Often on a Sunday morning Selma walked with our boarders into the open outskirts to have picnics under the pines. Sometimes they took the tramway on trips to the Roman aqueducts. There our children would walk in the meadows and climb the terraced fields, reaching the mossy pastures by the riverside. They would gather wildflower, daisies, poppies, anemones, red tulips, or luscious ferns, and return loaded with bouquets, which Selma took care in arranging. There was never a day in the year when Selma's office was empty of flowers. Always the tomboy in our family, with a straight, graceful figure, Selma never lost her love for the outdoors. She inherited our father's sense of humor, which helped us through many a crisis. Across the years there would be days when we had to carry youngsters to the hospital without their parents' knowledge, and days when it was difficult to find a doctor for an acute condition. There would be days when our budget did not meet the increasing cost of food and necessities, and days when fighting seemed at our doorsteps. I do not know what I would have done without Selma.

Ahliah continued to win the support of the middle classes and a small number of the upper-middle class who came from Syria and Palestine. To them, we were not so much threatening French interests as we were training the youth of Arab lands to have the dedication necessary for a purposeful life. At times our chances of survival seemed poor. I emphasized the morning assemblies as gatherings through which our girls learned to express themselves and know the meaning of human solidarity. As I recall the past, these morning gatherings stand out as the most precious experience of my educational career. Our students grew to be internationalists, familiar with the fights for freedom in many parts of the world. Across the years they contributed as much as they could to United Nations efforts to combat hunger, disease, fear, and disaster. As the problems of the Arab world struck deeply into their lives, they kept a fire of hope burning.

XIV

∾

ALMOST EVERYTHING about our lives was precarious, even when we were not noticing. The school developed. I took lovely holidays. Life was not all grimness and foreboding. But here is a letter one of our Palestinian boarding students, a nine-year-old named Jad, wrote home in 1937:

> *Dear Parents,*
> *Please come back soon. They say the road is going to be cut and we will not see you again. I will kill myself if I don't see you again.*

What is most painful about the letter is that it was not unique. Very few parents sent replies that could give their children peace of mind. Usually, sweets and money came instead. Only in retrospect is the imminence of catastrophe so unmistakable.

That spring of 1937, a temporary lull hovered over Palestine, and I made plans with friends from Haifa to visit the mysterious city of Petra, hidden in a valley south of Jerusalem. In a taxi driving through Haifa an American acquaintance spoke with great concern of the fast-developing harbor area. "You should not allow the Jews to take all of this away from you," he said. "You Arabs are intelligent people. You have contributed a lot to make this port modern; I have seen your laborers at work by the thousands. Do you believe you can retain Palestine by negotiations while your opponents prepare for war?" Later he told my hosts, the Boutagys, that they were risking a lot building their new hotel on Mount Carmel. "We are not afraid," Mrs. Boutagy said, radiant and smiling. "There is a God in heaven. There is a conscience in the world. We know that justice will triumph some day."

Ever since Hitler had come to power, throngs of people from several persecuted minorities had been fleeing to the Arab world. If they did not come by sea, they came via Turkey. From a human point of view, we were worried about them and felt it our duty to offer them hospitality. But the numbers began exceeding expectations, and we felt driven into a difficult situation. In 1935 alone 60,000 Jewish immigrants came to Palestine, a number equal to the entire Jewish population there at the end of World War I.

"Why doesn't England take them?" exclaimed some European friends.

"Nobody wants them," we answered.

Indeed, nobody did want them. The few countries willing to take Jews imposed strict quotas: only fifteen thousand were allowed into Australia over a period of three years; only one thousand were allowed into Rhodesia. Britain and America had small quotas. Uganda was regarded as a possibility for resettlement, but Zionists had organized strong networks in Palestine. People came legally or, often, illegally, and the West abdicated all responsibility.

The Boutagys could not contemplate the extent of that abdication. I doubt any of us could. And it was spring. Palestine was beautiful. The morning after the exchange with the American, eight of us climbed into the Boutagys' new station wagon and headed for Jerusalem. When we arrived there, the terrace of the King David Hotel looked gay with red and green umbrellas on the lawn, and we stopped for refreshments. Around us we heard many languages. German and English predominated. Jerusalem, indeed, was a microcosm of the world, with all its greed, jealousies, prejudices, and suspicions. Faces in the crowds were tense. People in traditional and modern dress jostled one another, their voices dissonant in many tongues.

To get to Petra we took a route via the Dead Sea, through the barren hills into Transjordan. There was little life until we came to Jericho, an oasis in a scorching valley where excavators were searching for Arab palaces. As we drove on, the hills became green, blooming with yellow and pink flowers. In the ruins of Jerash, once a wealthy trading city, we met shepherds who insisted that King Solomon had built this miraculous place. Yet there was the temple of Zeus, still surrounded by the ruins of four splendid theaters. A little beyond, on a promontory, stood the temple of Artemis, patroness of the city. We pressed on to Amman, where we took refreshments in the gardens of the Philadelphia Hotel. Lean sheep were searching for weeds and grass along the dusty steps of a Roman amphitheater. The shepherds looked exhausted, stretched out on the lower seats. How different was that picture from imagined scenes of Roman chariots racing over the field with captives facing death at the hands of the conquerors!

The next day, in the small town of Madaba, we encountered a Danish archaeologist studying a sixteenth-century mosaic map of ancient Palestine that formed the floor of a church. The map's fragments depicted the streets of Jerusalem lined with columns and golden fish swimming in the blue waters of the Jordan River. We drove off through the desert following the tracks of the old Hejaz railway, watching migrating birds race across the open sky. In the distance camel caravans were crossing toward Sinai on their way to Egypt or Arabia. By early afternoon we reached Al Karak, where the children's blue eyes and fair hair gave evidence of a great deal of intermarriage between the Crusaders and the Arabs. There is a saying, attributed to the Crusaders who populated the area nine hundred years before: "Why should we go back to the West when the East is so generous? In this land of sunshine and delicious vines let us make our permanent home."

Finally we arrived in Alji, gateway to the valley of Petra. We mounted horses and mules to traverse the gorge known by the name Sik. Colossal rocks formed walls on either side. We rode through a gorge, fascinated by its striated hues from pink to deepest rose. For more than an hour we rode until suddenly the narrow path opened up, and we came into the valley. Ahead of us a breathtaking facade adorned with columns and statues had been sculpted into a cliff. "This is the Treasury," exclaimed our guide, "the most enchanting of all the ruins." Six graceful columns supported the lower part of the unique structure; another six supported the upper floor. After admiring the building, we road our weary horses down the valley toward the central part of the dead city of Petra. Sunset colors wrapped the pinnacles in purple. We had a delicious meal of rice, olives, and dates in a spacious and colorful tent, then slept in caves that were once tombs.

German travelers had unveiled the ruins of Petra in 1812. Our guide, Abu Rayya, claimed that his ancestors had been the first to conduct the Germans across Palestine's desert roads. "Now you came most of the way by car, but at that time there were only horses, mules, and camels," he said. "There was no railway across Sinai, as there is now. Travelers rode animals slowly through the dangerous land."

Abu Rayya waited as we ate our breakfast. The dates in his pocket were enough to carry him through the day. He led us up the steep cliffs beyond the towering rocks to show us carvings in the red sandstone. On and on we climbed, up an enticing staircase to El Deir. Eight columns adorned the facade of the Deir Temple. Its great portico, thirty feet high, opened into large chambers. Abu Rayya told us that here the people had sacrificed sheep to their God. The next day we visited the Acropolis, more than three thousand feet above sea level, its tombs and altars carved into the rosy rock. Gazing across the desert, we could trace the great distance beyond Sinai. In that desolation the prophets heard God's voice, yet there we were amid the remains of pagan monuments. Centuries of monotheism had not obliterated them.

We rode the horses out of Petra and back through the twisting gorge, then drove south to the Red Sea. The sand stretched in dunes ahead of us. Desert birds and animals hid themselves in thick shrubbery or behind rocks. In Aqaba we took rooms in a modest hotel built by the army. Fishing boats were returning to the beach at sundown. Four miserable children came begging for corn. At nightfall they retired to their mud huts, and we took to narrow, uncomfortable beds. The breeze rustled the palms and waves broke against the pebbles while army guards whispered in the silence. In the morning the beach glistened with shells far more beautiful than any that one could find on the Mediterranean shores. Children in rags peddled strings of shell necklaces. Who would believe that from these shores Phoenician sailors piloted Solomon's navy into the Indian Ocean? From here mariners sailed into Ophir, fetching gold, silver, jewels, and rose water. We left the desert land and moved on to Beersheba, where verdure reappeared, and from there we drove back to the coastal cities of Palestine. Colorless flat houses were springing up. Strangers from the four corners of the world, not only refugees, had been urged to settle throughout the Holy Land.

The lull that had set in when we began our holiday could not last. We returned to Lebanon, and Palestine was aflame again. A hundred minor clashes between its Arab inhabitants and the Jewish émigrés had prepared the way. The Arabs, by far the majority, felt themselves being maneuvered into a corner. Only small portions of the land had been sold to Zionists, but these were well dispersed through the country, upsetting the equilibrium of the population. A spirit of ruthlessness, born of past suffering, was at work. Thousands of persecuted Polish and German Jews were using every device to establish themselves permanently in the Holy Land. As it was impossible to buy much land, they monopolized trade, industry, and the professional fields. At first, this seemed a legitimate way of making a life, but beneath this activity were secret schemes for expansion through war.

Rumors spread that vast quantities of arms were being accumulated by the Zionists and the British in the Tiberias area. Meanwhile, the British did not allow the Arabs to carry arms in self-defense. A colleague of ours from the university was suspected of carrying arms and was jailed. While in jail, he died mysteriously. For six months in 1936 the Arabs had gone on a general strike, and life was paralyzed. They thought their passive resistance might draw the attention of the world to their plight. By 1937 frustration led people to armed revolt, and the British to repression. Many young men were brutally carried off to prisons, and some were flogged to death. Turbulence during the strike and the ensuing revolt drove a number of wealthy families into Lebanon.

Late that summer, en route to an international conference in Geneva, three of us representing the Arab countries—one from Syria, one from Palestine, and I from Lebanon—decided to submerge our surface differences to focus on the problem of Palestine. When we arrived, Geneva seemed more serene than any European metropolis. Around us people of all nations mingled in the quiet squares and watched swans gliding on the water. Lake Geneva rippled gently along the fringe of green parks and gardens, while the cypresses of Rousseau's island swayed in the distance.

Because the University of London was sponsoring the gathering, English was supposed to be our common language, but there were times when it seemed we were marooned on the Tower of Babel. The Austrians, the Czechs, the Hungarians, and the Bulgarians quarreled in German; the Scandinavians, the largest geographical group, intervened using the same language. Translating some of the bitter arguments into milder English, they tried to restore an atmosphere of calm. Even they were restless, though, especially the Danes.

Our delegation tried to explain to our European friends how distressed we were about Jewish persecution in Europe, and also how unjust we felt it was that the Arab world was being forced to bear the consequences of Europe's cruelties. The Europeans were too engrossed with their own problems to pay much attention to us. The only German member of the conference, who lived in Switzerland, was treated with suspicion. The British, who formed a large delegation, were vexed by the popularity of the Scandinavians. Together with the French, they poked fun at the Italians. The conference convinced me that European youth had no serious leadership.

Their sarcasm and cynicism reflected the fear and moral fee-
bleness of a continent divided.

It was September as we prepared to leave. Every European
country, we were told, was increasing its armaments. We visited
the League of Nations as it was drawing its last breath. No
sooner had we embarked on our journey home than news of the
civil war in Spain reached us. Frightened refugees swarmed
round railway stations. Meanwhile, in Palestine, the Arab Revolt exploded. When we stopped for an interlude in Venice, the
city seemed unaware of any fighting. It felt timeless there,
peaceful. As we resumed our travels eastward through the
Balkans, though, hearts were heavy. No one wanted another
bloody war, and no one would avoid it.

Back home, the boarding students from Palestine at the
Ahliah School continued writing terrified letters home. Many
of their people were exiled, many killed or locked in prisons.
Outside the Arab world no one paid much attention as the
British swelled their ground troops, used their air force, and
armed Jewish settlers to suppress the Arab Revolt. Between
1936 and 1939 British firing squads executed more than a hundred Arabs. Some five thousand were killed; three to four times
as many were wounded. For a time in 1938 it seemed every day
brought news of another bomb in a cafe or market in Palestine.
Nothing was safe.[1]

I vacationed in Syria with my family two last times in those
years. In the spring of 1938, we visited the ancient city of Antioch and walked along the banks of the Orontes River in the late
afternoon, cutting through splendid fields and fruit orchards
on the outskirts, traveling to the gardens of laurels and gush-
ing waters where pagans believed Apollo pursued Daphne
until she implored Jupiter to turn her into a laurel tree. To the
Western powers, Antioch in 1938 was a "gift" to be handed over

to Turkey in return for the latter's loyalty to the Allies. To us it was part of the motherland. In slicing off a big portion of northern Syria to secure their new ally, Britain and France worried little about the families being separated and the properties being subdivided and sold.

That summer we drove between Damascus and Sueda through a boundless stretch of plains golden with wheat and cereals. We saw wild Arabian horses dashing across fields and heard the beat of their hooves all day while strolling amid the black stone dwellings of Sueda. As legend goes, the Arabian horse was tamed and bred by the sons of Noah, then found its way to Egypt, where its blood mingled with that of other horses. It is said the Romans raced it in Italy and England. On the Syrian plains the Arabian horse has remained purest. The rhythm of its hooves evoked in me a memory of some twenty years before, when we heard that the Arab cavalry had liberated Damascus and I, a child then, imagined a world made new.

*All photos courtesy
of Mariam C. Said
unless otherwise noted.*

Wadad Makdisi Cortas's parents,
Mariana and Jirjus

Wadad Makdisi Cortas and three of her
five siblings. Standing, from left to right:
Selma, Jirjus, Wadad. Seated, from left
to right: Fuad, Mariana, Bahige.

Interior of Wadad Makdisi's
childhood home

Sitto Mariam Cortas, Wadad's mother-in-law. Wadad refers to her in the text as Mother Cortas.

Wadad's sister
Soumaya

Wadad's brother Elias

Ahliah School graduates on a picnic, 1927. Wadad is third from left.

Graduation from American University of Beirut, 1930. Wadad is standing second from right.

Wadad Makdisi and Emile Cortas's wedding

Wadad Makdisi Cortas giving
a talk on the radio

Wadad Makdisi Cortas
leaning against the family car

Wadad and Mona, her cousin and
sister-in-law

Wadad's sister Selma

Wadad and Emile in England, 1952

Wadad and her daughter, Mariam

Wadad with her children. Mariam is playing the piano, in the background from left to right are Ramzi and Nadim, and Sami is standing in front of Wadad.

Wadad with her three sons, from left to right Sami, Ramzi, and Nadim

The four children, 1949, on the balcony of the Beirut apartment. Clockwise from the top: Sami, Nadim, Mariam, and Ramzi

Wadad Makdisi Cortas in her office at school

Wadad Makdisi Cortas sitting with colleagues in the school courtyard

Morning assembly at the Ahliah School for Girls

The choir of the Académie Libanaise des Beaux-Arts. The girls are students from the Ahliah School. Wadad Makdisi Cortas is standing next to the conductor, Alexis Boutros.

Ballet class at the Ahliah School for Girls

Mariam with her mother at her graduation from the Ahliah School, 1959

A graduation ceremony at the Ahliah School for Girls

Exterior of the Ahliah School for Girls. This is the building in which Wadad was a student, a teacher, and then a principal for forty years. Photo courtesy of Rayya Haddad.

A graduation ceremony. In the front row, third from left, is Wadad's Uncle Anis Makdisi, the poet, and sixth from left is her brother-in-law Constantine Zurayk.

Wadad, Helen Keller, and her companion Polly Thompson on stage at a school assembly

Mariam's graduating class from elementary school

Front entrance to the
Ahliah School for Girls

Wadad and Emile Cortas on holiday in Athens, 1971

Three generations of women: Wadad, Najla, and Mariam, 1977

Wadad with her grandchildren Najla and Samer, who was born in 1976

A Cortas family gathering at Christmas in 1972. Of particular interest are, in the back row, fifth from left: Constantine Zurayk; sixth from left: Emile Cortas. Seated, fourth from left: Wadad Makdisi Cortas; fifth from left: Edward Said holding Wadie; and Mariam Said at far right.

The house at Brummana. Photo courtesy of Rayya Haddad.

The Ahliah School for Girls, 2009. Photo courtesy of Rayya Haddad.

The Cortas family, 1968. Standing, from left to right: Mariam, Sami, Wadad, Ramzi, and Nadim; seated: Emile.

XV

❧

ONE MORNING IN 1938 the doorbell rang to announce an
unexpected visitor. I was envisioning a soldier with some
directive when the gateman ushered in a young man whom I
vaguely knew as a prosperous architect in town. He was looking, he said, for a place where he could gather a few musicians
to play the classics. He had founded an association of young
people interested in music called the Association of Amateur
Musicians. I was not altogether in the mood to pay attention,
but his conviction in advancing something positive had a sooth-
ing effect on my tired nerves. I listened intently and found myself agreeing to help him. I could spare a small space; he was
welcome to use it.

"You can start tonight if you wish," I said. There were just
three of them at first. My new friend the architect played the
cello, a young lady teacher played the piano, and a medical student played the violin. They labored over a Beethoven trio. Before the evening ended, they tried Handel's "Largo."

As the days progressed, the participants became more numerous, especially after some of our girls were introduced to
classical music. In order to involve everyone interested, it was

necessary to have more singing. What a blessed moment it was when our girls came onto the scene in force in 1939 and added their energy and voices! Soon we had about eighty people in the choir, and before the year ended the musical association had more than 150 members.

We held small chamber concerts at the Ahliah School and other places and prepared for our first major public concert, in May 1940, at the American University's Assembly Hall. On the day of that concert, news came that the French general in charge of Lebanon had been summoned urgently to France. The country was in danger of falling to the Nazis, and our people, under French control for thirty years, were despondent. The heavenly music of Haydn's *Creation* and Handel's *Messiah* was a temporary refuge.

As war thundered through Europe and North Africa, I was anxious about the few boarders entrusted to our care and the 150 day students. Although Beirut was in no way a target, we were ordered by the authorities to build shelters and teach our students how to escape immediate peril. On June 14, 1940, within weeks of our concert, France capitulated. Its fall brought conflict to Syria and Lebanon. More battleships moved toward our coast, and planes buzzed in our skies. Orders came from Marshal Pétain that the Vichy armistice stipulated the complete surrender of the French Mandates. The Nazi army did not march on Beirut, but the country was opened to German and Italian secret service men. There was a period of great fear.

Despite the Vichy quislings, the government of France in exile continued to exercise influence over us. On June 8, 1941, we were notified that it was wise to shutter the schools. French nationalist forces under Gen. Charles de Gaulle were marching with the British army from Palestine to occupy Lebanon and Syria. Life constricted as schools and colleges closed. Anyone who was able left the city for the mountains. From June to early July the Lebanese coast was bombarded. Villages on the outskirts of the capital were terrorized by night raids. When the operations were over, the British and Free French triumphantly entered Beirut. At the front of the parade was General de Gaulle, whose imposing height impressed the assembled masses cheering the army. Its arrival gave confidence to the people, who had thought that France had disappeared from the scene, leaving the country defenseless.

School resumed along with our musical activities, but as the latter expanded, we had difficulties with the authorities, for mass gatherings were an object of suspicion. One day in January of 1942, two policemen rang the school bell to arrest our choirmaster.

"What for?" we asked.

"For failing to secure a teaching permit. He is an architect, and we understand he is engaged in teaching music."

When they discovered that the man had no financial interest in the matter and was willing to teach whoever came to him, one of them said, "Although I came to arrest you, sir, could you take me as a pupil?" This policeman eventually became one of the most regular attendants, confirming my belief that we can detest imperialism but music is another domain. We did secure a permit, and ultimately we merged our association into the Lebanese Academy of Fine Arts. All through the war the girls and boys and men and women of our musical group rehearsed long hours and under strict control, preparing for concerts. Between 1943 and 1946, these concerts attracted Allied soldiers from the frontiers of Palestine and Syria. A few asked to join in the singing, and we took them in happily. A middle-aged colonel from South Africa was among them. One Sunday morning he came for a rehearsal of Mendelssohn's *Elijah*, crushed by news of the disappearance of his sixteen-year-old daughter. When the choir joined in "Lift thine eyes, O lift thine eyes to the mountains," he sang lustily. I shall never forget his voice that day or the calm dignity with which he left after the rehearsal.

There was also a soldier from England who had trained as a musician and who became one of our leading soloists. His discipline helped put our inexperienced soloists on the right track. Thanks to him, we also got a great deal of musical literature when communications with Europe were unreliable. An extremely talented Jewish musician named Castle, who had fled from Munich, joined in many of our choral concerts. His solo part in Handel's "Pastoral" symphony was of rare quality. Zionism held no appeal for Castle, and when the war was over he found a welcoming job in one of the leading orchestras in the States. It was glorious to share the immortal music with such men, to relieve them briefly from the horrors of war. It was a moving experience in the spring of 1945 to sing *Elijah* in Jerusalem, accompanied by the Palestine Broadcasting System Orchestra. The choir would travel to other cities in Palestine, and later to Egypt, Syria, and Turkey. We would sing in concert halls and hospitals, in schools, and even in the few open-air theaters. Many years later, after the catastrophe, we would visit old Jerusalem, bringing something beautiful to Arab people torn by grief and suffering in one of the most tragic cities of the world.

XVI

～

B ACK IN THE DAYS when I was still in high school, my brother
Elias had a friend who came often to our house. Emile Cortas was a tall, dark young Quaker with a courteous manner and
honest black eyes. Sometimes he and my brother would overhear
me when I was in one of my romantic moods, reciting poetry in
what I thought was privacy. The boys would tease me about these
literary flights. There was an easy fellowship between us; Emile
came to be one of our household's wide circle of friends.

In the first year of the war, my friendship with Emile was renewed. We found that the years had given us much in common,
and when the question of marriage arose, I felt sure. It was like
coming home.

We were married on July 20, 1940, in his home village of Brummana. Our wedding ceremony took place in the Quaker Meeting
House, surrounded by pines and cypress trees. Our choir sang a
"Gloria" by Mozart and a few traditional hymns, and then we
made our vows to each other in the manner of the Friends.

My new family consisted of a father, mother, and younger
brother. Two happily married daughters lived in our neighborhood. Emile's parents had known rewarding lives working and

teaching in the Quaker mission school, which had been built, along with a hospital, in the last part of the nineteenth century by a Swiss missionary named Waldemeier. Emile's mother, around sixty, was a gracious lady whose personality was more forceful than her husband's. During World War I the two of them maintained a humanitarian center for the poor villages. Money came from the United States, and hundreds of women and children were given food and shelter. As a boy, my husband cut short his schooling to help his parents in this project. When that war was over, he was sent to Beirut to resume his studies, while the parents continued on with re-established Quaker institutions.

Emile worked his way through university, laboring at night and at odd hours to gain on lost time. The subject of his BA thesis was fruit preservation in Lebanon, a topic that was to become his life's interest. As he had no capital, he started in the fruit industry on a very small scale, preparing a limited quantity of jams with his mother's help. When he had some savings, he made a trip to Ireland, where he worked at Dublin's Lamb jam factory. Upon his return he widened the scope of his operation, giving security to the family.

Our country house in Brummana was a beautiful old residence surrounded by grapevines, apricots, and red and white oleanders. The arcaded pillars of the porch were entwined with red roses, ivy, and morning glory. The entrance hall ceiling was supported by old pine beams and led into rooms outfitted with books and rugs and comfortable chairs.

Brummana nestled peacefully amid a large forest of pine and oak. Below its red-tiled roofs stretched valleys and foothills reaching to the open sea. At sunset the whole area appeared to glow in a purple mist. My husband and I stayed there through the fighting in the summer of 1941. After de Gaulle's triumph, the old Quaker school had to give up its premises to the army. In fact, all of Brummana became a military base. Lebanon and Syria were then governed by a tripartite authority. The military command was in the hands of the British; the French high commissioner was trying to re-establish the power of the Mandate, even though independence had been formally proclaimed on November 26, 1941. A Lebanese government headed by President Alfred Georges Naccache attempted to bring life to normal.

An Australian unit was stationed in the area. We entertained groups of these men in our home. Many of them were driven to war against their convictions. They had no chance to escape it. Many told us how their families, tired of war, had left Europe for Australia in 1920. I remember one particularly sad-looking chap. His name was Sebastian Bach, descendant of the great Bach. After World War I, he told me, "My father, like all young Germans then, was longing for peace. Our nation bled to pay a frightful indemnity. Both the French and the British were ruthless with us. What was needed then was to disarm not Germany alone but all the mighty nations."

"Why are you fighting with the British?" I asked.

"They are the best of a bad lot," he answered.

Sebastian had recently learned that his wife had lost their first-born baby. He sang with us, and I hope our chorus gave him a measure of relief from despair.

The Australians had fought in Greece in the spring of 1941 and were forced to surrender to the Germans with other Allied forces. At that time Greek refugees came to Beirut, settling in convents or hotels and living on British rations. One cold December day I was in a store when a Greek woman came in holding her three-year-old by the hand. She had a tin of jam, which she wanted to trade for a sweater for the boy. Overhearing her, a British officer went into a fury, grabbed the jam from her, and shouted, "My wife and children are being deprived of sugar to give it to you, and you go selling your rations away!" He disappeared in his jeep, leaving the woman bemoaning her loss.

A few days later I was at the school when the radio reported the attack on Pearl Harbor. The Allied stations minimized the damage, while German and Italian radio spoke of the heroism of the Japanese. It was a terrible sensation, I remember, sitting in my office, pondering the sorrows of this war. Our first child, a lovely little daughter, was born two weeks later. We named her Mariam, and her coming brought great joy into this dark period.

All through that winter we had open house for members of the Friends' Ambulance Unit. They were young men who bore no arms and refused to fight. Some later lost their lives collecting wounded soldiers from the battlefield. Army officers also came to our home. Usually they sat sipping drinks and talking business with my husband till the late hours. I joined this group on only one occasion. There were two army men and two German refugees living in Palestine. The latter were full-fledged Zionists and spoke with assurance of the near future when three million to four million of them would settle in the Holy Land. Although they had been in Haifa for a few years, they knew remarkably little about the rest of the country. One had not even been to Jerusalem.

I argued with them as logically as I could, pointing out that the population of Palestine had been predominantly Arab for more than a thousand years. I presented statistical tables prepared by the British Mandate showing that despite the exodus and all the territorial purchases and illegal migration since 1920, the Jews possessed only 5 percent of the total land in the country. Statistics in no way interested them. They knew that the big powers were behind the Zionists. They knew the Arabs of Palestine had no armies or oil wealth. Our guests shamelessly spoke of war and terrorism. They plainly stated that the Zionists would justify any means in pursuit of their ends. Neither my husband nor I could sleep that night. Such brash talk right at our dinner table made us feel as helpless as infants.

In the summer of 1942, we returned to Brummana to find that our house, like so many in the village, had been requisitioned by the Allied forces. We found residence on a hilltop, but the valleys were no longer quiet. With every sunrise and for hours through the day we heard the echo of drill masters shouting at young recruits being trained to use their guns. Our daughter, Mariam, six months old, slept sweetly, undisturbed in her pram under the pines. When the summer was over, we went again to Beirut.

We followed the war's progress on the radio. The bombing of the Italian coast. The raids over German and British cities. The battles of Tobruk and El Alamein. And we followed it with each fresh wave of immigrants to Beirut. Russians, Romanians, Poles, and others came. A young Russian nun taught French at our school. When she wasn't teaching, she led her church choir. After her first year with us, she laid aside her white habit and came to me dressed in an attractive red ensemble. She had decided to become a nightclub singer! It turned out she had a pathetic love story. As a refugee at Prague University, she had met a young compatriot, and the two had fled to Turkey and then Jerusalem. There they joined the religious orders, for a sense of security, she said, and also because they thought it wise to try living in a new way before binding themselves in marriage. When their probation was over, her friend decided to remain in the order. She was torn by conflicting ideas and came to Beirut.

Her friends were saddened, even alarmed, by her decision to work at a nightclub, but who could blame her when her hopes had faded away? Another Russian member of our staff, Alexis, was an expert on French culture and eventually became an authority on the Crusades and our own country. Alexis was extremely anti-Communist and romantic about the czarist past. When the Russians entered the war on the side of the Allies, I teased him, "Are you still a white Russian now?" to which he replied, "I am neither white nor red; I am only pink."

My father-in-law would spend the whole day listening to the BBC. Although he too had no sympathy for the Soviets, he thrilled when they finally defeated the Germans at Stalingrad, in February of 1943. He could not know then, as no one could, how devastating Stalingrad and the war on the Eastern Front would be to the German army. Though the Russians' victory there cheered him, he listened to the radio with a general sense of gloom. Back in 1941 he would look at a map saying, "Crete, Crete. I have hopes in Crete, for it is rocky and difficult to approach. The British know it well." When the radio had announced news of the Allied surrender of Crete, he had nailed himself to the wireless. Thousands of German parachutists had dropped on the tiny island. In little more than a week, the Allies were overwhelmed. To my father, this invasion was an interesting landmark in history; nothing of the sort had ever happened. Afterward he could not feel optimistic about Lebanon's future, but he still hoped for an Allied victory. However, to my father-in-law, the fall of Crete was the end of his hopes. After that, he never failed to tune in to the BBC, waiting impatiently every morning for Churchill's voice. He listened to every speech and quoted every dramatic word. But his health started deteriorating from that point.

In early April of 1943, our son Nadim was born, bringing another ray of hope. That same spring my father-in-law died. His remains rest in the Friends cemetery in Brummana. In the end, he was right about Crete, though he would never know it. The Germans had lost almost seven thousand parachutists taking the island, ruining their chance of launching an airborne invasion of the Soviet Union and delaying that invasion by many weeks. So, in a sense, Stalingrad was the price for Crete, "a disastrous victory," as one German general put it.

XVII

༄

THE ENORMOUS MILITARY FORCE stationed in the Middle
East during World War II brought a boom to Lebanon. It
was an artificial boom, but there was new wealth and people
started thinking about opportunities after the war. Our highest
national aspirations involved elections and a new Parliament.
Despite a formal proclamation of the end of its Mandate in
1941, France would not transfer power to a Lebanese government until 1943 and would maintain an armed presence until
1946. For some of us, having an autonomous national university at the dawn of independence was more important than having an army, an air force, or any military organization. And in
the early years of the war, a group of educators often met at our
home to discuss the possibility of starting such a university.

We were all infinitely grateful for foreign universities on our
soil but equally conscious of the necessity of having our own institutions. Foreign (particularly French) influence had made
progress in education slow and difficult. Instruction was in
French or English but not Arabic. "Arabic is not culturally up to
standard" was the argument. Anything that inspired love of
country or language, or drew us nearer to other Arab countries,

had been discouraged by our colonizers; any movement that bred self-respect was refuted and killed in its infancy. The same desire for freedom of thought expressed by the Algerians, Egyptians, Syrians, and other North Africans applied to us.

Our group started with seven and expanded to twelve. Discussion went something like this: Maurice Chehab, an archaeologist, argued the value of a national university for expanding his field of expertise. Foreigners, he said, have not done much digging in Lebanon. The descendant of a family that ruled Lebanon during one of its great periods, he was aware of the treasures hidden in its earth and enthusiastic about renewing scientific excavation. Alexis Boutros, the architect who was central in forming our musical association, insisted that in a postcolonial society a concentration in architecture would be critical for propelling a Lebanese university. The same was true, said the historian Constantine Zurayk and others, of a broad base in the study of the humanities.[1] Anis Freiha, an Arab linguist, spoke of expanding vistas of folklore research. He was busy collecting the legends of Lebanon, as well as recording scenes of rural life that were vanishing under the pressure of Western culture. "And what of law?" Edmond Rabbath, a lawyer from Syria, proposed, saying that legal studies in Arabic would surely be essential. Likewise the need to train young people for government posts, said Negib Sadaka, a diplomat of high standing.

Ideas surged among these sincere, talented men, but some were called away, and the end of the war would disperse the group further. Boutros had the daring and the financial means to take the initial steps. We settled at the start for three schools of fine arts. Fine arts do not frighten colonial powers. The Lebanese Academy officially started as an institution for higher education on March 15, 1943. Its School of Architecture was inaugurated by Michel Ecochard, a French urbanist who lived in Algiers for the major part of his life. His address at the opening was admirable for both its deep respect for Arabs' architectural heritage and its intelligent assimilation of modern trends. A large group of Lebanese and Syrian young men registered for the school's first year.

Meanwhile, Cesar Gemayel and a group of Lebanese painters organized a School of Painting and Sculpture. There were only a few applicants at first; then the number doubled and tripled, and pretty soon Gemayel and his collaborators were training more than a hundred young artists. The sculptor Alfred Basbous was one of our graduates, as were the celebrated Lebanese painters Omar Onsi and Mustafa Farroukh.

The Academy's third school was dedicated to what was a life passion for many of our group: music. The choral group that we had formed as the Association of Amateur Musicians became the basis of the Academy's orchestra and choir and continued to perform concerts and train young musicians. Dance was later added as one of the school's concentrations.

In 1945 the Academy moved into the heart of Beirut. A convent built in the seventeenth century was remodeled to fit our needs. Students came not only from Lebanon but from Syria, Egypt, Iraq, and Turkey. The architects in particular found rewarding jobs with their respective governments, engaging in city planning in the developing countries of the Arab world. In 1948, when the UNESCO Conference was to be held in Beirut, the Academy, in agreement with the Ministry of Education, took the occasion to initiate a four-year course for teachers who were unable to leave their jobs to specialize abroad. Negib Sadaka ultimately developed a four-year degree program in political studies and economics.

If the Lebanese Academy played a limited role in our cultural life, it was certainly a pioneering role. In its search for an identity, Lebanon was awakened to the importance of liberal education in the hands of its own people.

XVIII

∾

C OL. WILLIAM EDDY, the first American ambassador in Saudi Arabia, told President Roosevelt in 1945, "Our Marshall Plan can only be carried out with Arab oil."

"Don't worry," Roosevelt is said to have answered, "we are wise enough not to antagonize the Arabs. Moreover, King Saud is a wise empire builder. He can see the advantages of our proposals, and we can see the advantages of his oil." This was not to be a bargain for justice.

In March of 1945 the Arab League was formed. It included Syria, Lebanon, Egypt, Iraq, Jordan, Saudi Arabia, and Yemen. No one spoke of Palestine then. It was still under the British Mandate. In the same year the three Allied leaders met in Yalta in the Crimea with the intent of determining the spoils of victory. Stalin, Roosevelt, and Churchill decided to divide Germany and partition Berlin. Many of us thought that Roosevelt was impartial in dealing with the Palestinian problem. We were disheartened when he died and the Arab League proved to be weak, swayed by whims and dissension.

In Palestine, terrorism had governed since 1944. That year the British High Commissioner was attacked by the Haganah, which the British had supported and armed only a few years earlier. In 1944 Lord Moyne, the British ambassador in Cairo, was assassinated. Attacks on police stations in Palestine occurred daily. Smuggling was prevalent, and munitions were stolen from the army camps. In 1946 the King David Hotel was dynamited; almost a hundred people died. Menachem Begin, the head of the Irgun terrorist organization and later prime minister of Israel, declared, "We must always take the offensive. Out of blood, fire, and ashes, a new specimen of human being is born. Whether we like it or not, there are a million Arabs who live in Palestine. Their war against us will be long. They already possess the land." So it was that from March of 1947 onward, the Irgun and Stern terrorists committed a series of murderous attacks on Arab villages and towns, killing civilians by the hundreds.

British forces were still responsible for the security of Palestine, but they did not intervene to crush the Zionists as they had crushed the Arab Revolt ten years earlier. Rather, they announced they would evacuate within a year, without providing any plan for the country's future. (By contrast to the French in Lebanon, the British had never set up any semblance of a local government in Palestine to operate as a junior partner with the British Mandate.) More and more Palestinians fled, and as our school year began in October, we received more of their terrified children.

A fourteen-year-old girl named Samia wrote her parents that year:

> Uncle visits me every day. He always takes me to the cinema
> on Sunday but I miss you all. I would rather not see the
> cinema but see you. Will you come before the Jews set on fire
> the roads? They say there are no more cars and the railway
> road is dynamited. Can you come by boat? My friend Nuha

*said her family went to Egypt. She cries all the time, afraid
of not being able to see them again. Did you hear about
them or about her uncles? How terrible is war. I hate it
with all my heart. Can no one stop it? You once said the
English army can stop it. Is it true? Why don't they do so? I
have left in my drawer my golden watch. The pretty watch
you gave me last year. My album is there; please bring it
with you too. Please come even if you do not find the watch
and album. A girl told me that when the people search for
their things they find nothing. The Jews have stolen away
all the gold and silver. Is it true our house is now empty
and new people have taken possession of it?*

The Zionists were openly carrying out arms deals with
Czechoslovakia and the Western countries at this time. "During
the fighting, Israel secured fifty of the most modern fighter aircraft from Czechoslovakia," reported Colonel Eddy. "I do not
recall that any U.S. congressmen or editors denounced this arms
traffic. Fifty jets will not kill the U.S. economy; only more Arabs
live or die. Who cares whether Arabs live or die?"

On November 29, 1947, the United Nations ratified the Partition Plan for Palestine. It called for the establishment of a Jewish state, an Arab state, and an international area around
Jerusalem. Fighting began almost immediately. Having won the
battle for world opinion, the Zionists expanded deeper into
Arab territories.[1]

Into this world of pain, my last baby was born, in December
1947. There were complications, and I had to be carried to the
hospital at midnight, but luckily my little boy was saved
through the best medical care available. We named him Sami.
We had four beautiful children now (my second little boy,
Ramzi, was born in 1945), and we were joyful. At the same time

I thought, What of the hundreds of mothers and mothers-to-be who were adrift in the wind, homeless, or living in bombarded cities, pursued by terrorism and violence?

In the early months of 1948 Arabs and Jews died in the streets. Bombings of crowded cafes and theaters, dynamiting of public buildings, looting—these were regular events. Many civilians were murdered in cold blood. On April 9 members of the Irgun, along with commandos from the Stern Gang and the Haganah, slaughtered 254 defenseless men, women, and children in the village of Deir Yassin.[2] They put twenty-five village men in lorries and paraded them around Jerusalem before taking them to a stone quarry, where the men were executed. This terrible incident created panic in many other Arab villages, and a large-scale exodus gained momentum. The same night the Irgun and Stern invited the foreign press for cookies and tea to explain their act as a necessary military operation.

Hassan, a Palestinian boy of twelve boarding with us at the Ahliah School, wrote to his parents:

> Omar the driver told me there is a fire all over Palestine. He said they have burnt the harbor in Jaffa and they have killed all the sailors. Jaffa is a sad place. There is war in the city and the people are running away into the villages. But even the villages are on fire. They are burning the trees. Please come before they block the road.

Jaffa had been designated an Arab city by the Partition Plan. The Irgun attacked it on April 25. Where there had been 55,000 Arab residents, only about 4,000 remained in Jaffa after the assault. On May 14, a day before the British Mandate expired, the Jews declared their state of Israel; then Arab armies attacked. On May 20 the UN appointed Count Folke Bernadotte to mediate a peace settlement. Building castles in the air about his wise plans, I was among many Arabs who believed, "Here comes a savior who will bring us out of darkness into light and justice."

I remember with what hopeful anxiety we followed his trip to Jerusalem. The Lebanese press was full of his news. While young Palestinians knocked at our door asking for help, recounting pitiful stories of lost homes and lost families, I remember looking into their despairing eyes and telling myself, "Never mind, all will be well again when Bernadotte comes." Like a child's faith, mine grew as I followed his mission. I knew his schedule by heart.

He was in Cairo at the end of May. In his first report Bernadotte stated with unsurpassed honesty that the Zionist forces had launched nearly 200 violent attacks on peaceful Arab towns. He could not ignore the fact that so long as the British were responsible for security, Arab troops had not entered Palestine. Bernadotte was given samples of the leaflets dropped by planes over Galilee saying, "All Palestinians who do not want war must leave, together with their women and children, in order to be safe. This is going to be a cruel war with no mercy or compassion."

In the early part of June, he made several trips to Haifa, Amman, and Cairo, before coming to Beirut. From Beirut, he went to Damascus. Early in July, he was in Rhodes. From Rhodes, he flew again to Jerusalem, for the last time. His assassination, on September 17, was like an earthquake. We heard the news on the radio. "Of course world opinion will not stand for this," we muttered among ourselves. Press accounts were blurry. Now, years later, there is no confusion. I take the liberty of quoting here from the account of his companion on that fateful day, Gen. Aage Lundstrom, which was included as an appendix to Bernadotte's posthumously published diary, *To Jerusalem*:

Count Bernadotte's white Dakota landed according to schedule at Beirut airport in the morning of September 16. After lunch with the Lebanese Prime Minister, the party proceeded to Damascus with the U.N.O. representatives. Here he was honorably received, and a magnificent piece of brocade was presented on this occasion. He said he looked forward to being able to give it to his wife for her birthday in a few days' time. It was actually the day of his funeral.

At 9.30 on Friday, 17th of September, we took off from Damascus to Jerusalem. The radio operator gave us a warning against landing at Kalandia Airport and stated that all aircraft landing would be fired at. We decided not to pay attention to it and landed without incident at 10.15. The Commander of the Arab Legion Force was there to meet us, together with a number of U.N.O. observers. I proposed that instead of crossing the Mandelbaum Gate we should enter Jerusalem from the West. This would take longer but would be safer. Bernadotte would have nothing to do with the proposal. "I have to take the same risks as my observers; if I do not go, I will be admitting that they have the right to prevent me from crossing the lines."

As we were approaching Jerusalem on our way back from Ramallah, our car was fired on but no one was hurt. When we got out a bullet had hit the hub of the left-hand rear wheel.

The sun shone from a cloudless sky. It felt quite fresh. Jerusalem is 800 metres above sea level. Few shots fell round us but we were protected behind a wall. One of the observers signalled with a large white flag from the tower for the guards to open the gate. We passed the Mandelbaum Gate without mishap and proceeded to the Y.M.C.A. headquarters of the observers on the Jewish side. Here, we were to spend the night. Both the Y.M.C.A. and the King David Hotel had been placed at the disposal of the U.N.O.

As snipers were very active there, I felt relieved when we passed the Jewish lines. The barrier was up, but when the [Jewish] guard saw us he let it down halfway, then drew it right up, and finally let it down completely. This forced us to stop. The Jewish liaison officer shouted something to the guard in Hebrew, after which he drew up the barrier completely, thus allowing us to pass.

It was suspected after the murder that mysterious manipulation of the barrier must have been a signal to the murderers that we were on our way, possibly indicating which car Bernadotte was travelling in. Just after passing the barrier, we met a few lorries full of Jewish soldiers and an armoured car in which the governor of the Jewish sector was riding.

The road ran now over a hill; just after we had cleared the top we were stopped by a jeep that barred the road. This jeep was larger than the Jewish Army jeep. It was suspected to have been stolen from the U.N.O. observers and painted brown. The driver appeared to be trying to turn it nervously, and in the end it stopped in the middle of the road. The four men in it were dressed in the khaki uniforms of the Jewish Army. Three of them jumped out and came towards our cars. Two on the right-hand side and one on the left; the driver remained in the jeep. Dr. Hillman called out something in Hebrew to let us pass. The third man ran past the two cars to our car. He, like the others, was armed with an automatic pistol. He peered at us through the window. We thought he wanted to inspect our passes and were prepared to take them out. He suddenly stuck the mouth of his pistol through the window and fired a burst of shots at Bernadotte and Serot [Col. Andre Serot, the chief UN observer in Jerusalem] from a few metres' range. It was now 5 p.m. After firing a few more shots, the man ran back towards the jeep. Colonel Bergly who jumped out to grapple with him was badly burnt in the face. The two other men opened fire on the wheels of the first car to prevent it following them. Then they jumped into the jeep which set off at top speed and disappeared.

The man who committed the murder did not have time to get into the jeep. Serot died immediately. Bernadotte bent as if he tried to shield himself. "Are you wounded?" I asked. He nodded and mumbled. Immediately afterwards he raised himself into a sitting position. We drove at great speed to the nearest hospital. We helped to carry the wounded. Serot had died instantaneously. He received 17 bullets. Bernadotte had received six bullets, one in the heart.

Next morning the murderers had sent a cable to France-Express expressing regret at the murder of Serot. Their intention had been to murder me instead in my capacity as Chief of Staff.[3]

XIX

〜

THE WOUNDS OF THE PALESTINIAN war never healed. Year after year we looked to the United Nations for a solution that never came. After Bernadotte's murder the Arab press declared, "The conscience of the world is dead." The Zionists' state had been quickly recognized by the West. A Jewish reporter later wrote:

Israel started its National Career by murdering one of the most beloved men of the world. . . . In vain the United Nations demanded that Israel bring the assassins to justice. Ben Gurion declared that the murderers cannot be found. . . . In December 1948, the United Nations resolved that all refugees wishing to return home would be permitted to do so at the earliest practicable date, and that compensation for the property of those who do not wish to return must be available. This resolution has been annually re-affirmed by the General Assembly, but nothing ever happened to implement it.

Israel defied every UN resolution and got by without being reprimanded. When Egypt signed the armistice with Israel, in

February 1949, Zionist troops moved beyond the demarcation line and annexed the Negev. Then they moved into Aqaba, where they clashed with the Arab Legion. No voice was heard from the United Nations to check the advance. More Arabs were made homeless as the Israelis annexed territories beyond the armistice line. How can we know what boundaries would satisfy Israel? It has never declared any.

A million refugees had their homes taken from them. When they fled, they could not have fathomed that they would not be allowed back but were doomed to live on charity. As Glubb Pasha, then commander in chief of the Arab Legion, wrote, "In 1940, great numbers of French people left their homes because of advancing German armies, but were allowed to get back. Nobody has ever suggested that they forfeited their right to return when the war was over. This [dispossession] lends to the Palestinian problem a desperate quality, and bears no resemblance to any other war in modern history."[1]

Palestine had been living on its nerves ever since the Balfour Declaration was made known, and from those girlhood days listening avidly to the conversation among my father's visitors, I never felt its travails were abstract. The trip between Haifa and Beirut was less than three hours by the coast road. People came and went, our lives entwined. But I had experienced a new depth of intimacy with Palestine since the 1930s, when its anxious mothers sent their children to our school.

The first group that came to us represented a cross-section of the middle-class population. From Haifa, two lovely girls and a boy, children of a hotel manager, were well bred and intelligent, good at sports and skilled at the piano. From Jaffa, we had a girl and boy of a doctor whose medical activities were expanding across the south. Within hardly a year his young wife was a widow, her husband shot dead while attending a patient in his hospital. A Jaffa government official sent his three daughters and a son; their younger cousins joined us a month later. Their father, an ardent nationalist, was pessimistic about his country's future and feared losing the orchards he had inherited from his grandparents. The people from Haifa tended to be optimistic. They said the Zionists could never outnumber the Arab population and seemed to know little of the political scheming behind the immigration policy. One father, an attorney general from Haifa, believed the International Court of Justice at The Hague would solve the Palestinian problem; his brother, a far less educated person, was skeptical.

A jeweler from Acre came to us with three daughters and a son. His wife and the girls were decked with gold bracelets and earrings and necklaces, insurance for the days to come. Very often in the late 1930s and early 1940s the mothers stayed in Beirut, while fathers moved back and forth across the border. I still remember the tears of a mother who brought her four daughters and a son to us. Occasionally she would stay late to see them tucked into bed. We had one sixteen-year-old Jewish girl whose family had emigrated from Germany to Jerusalem in 1939. Her father was a rabbi interested in writing commentaries on the Prophet Isaiah. Wrapped up in his religious studies, he was completely indifferent to the politics of Palestine. As the tension increased, he left Palestine and settled in Lebanon.

When fighting intensified and communication sometimes became impossible as people were dispersed, boarding schools in Jerusalem sent us many children without the knowledge of their parents. I cannot forget how these children would rouse in the night, screaming with fear, and would have to be held and comforted before they could sleep again. One morning three sweet girls, ages seven to ten, arrived with their aunt. They had no news whatsoever from their parents in Jaffa and were completely out of money. The girls looked frightened, and as the aunt expressed their anxiety, I was unable to hold back my tears. "Alas," she said, "I came to you to encourage these children and you burst into tears." I had children of my own about the same age, and the sight of these bewildered little creatures pained me beyond words.

A year or two before the catastrophe, I began setting down the stories of our boarders. By then, Palestinian children were being sent to us by the hundreds. When the parents could not accompany them, there was often a driver or faithful servant. In the spring of 1947 I met Hania, the servant of a rich Arab family in Tiberius. She was about twenty-nine but looked older. I asked her about life in Tiberius, but it was Acre, that forlorn city by the sea, that she wished to speak of.

Yes, it was in Acre, exactly ten years ago, that my brother was hanged. There near the Serail, he was imprisoned for six months, and then the news came. He and his three comrades were sentenced to death by the British.

It was a terrible thing to happen. A few months before, my eldest brother was shot dead as he was sniping at Jewish fighters from the hills. They called him a martyr, and the fact that he died fighting for his country gave my mother some consolation. With Omar, who was only nineteen, it was very painful. He was executed, and she could not abide that: "Why? Because he held his gun when the Jews rushed to dynamite houses in our village? Because he shot at them, and they fled?" This was during the Arab Revolt. British soldiers came and searched every house. They caught fifteen young men of our village who had arms and took them to Acre for judgment. For my mother, it was too heavy a burden. For days she refused to eat or drink. Finally she died.

After that Hania looked for work in Tiberius. Her three brothers were little, and her father needed help supporting them. When I met her, a battle was raging in Tiberius. Within a year the town would fall to the Zionists. "No one knows what might happen to us," she said. "I do not care anymore whether I live or die. But my brothers. . . . My father has lost his sight, and they are still too young to take care of themselves."

I could crowd this book with such stories. A boy of ten, who came to board in 1946, told me: "My uncle's house was the largest in the district of Galilee. It was beautiful, with a wide garden. The balconies opened to the lake. We often went there to spend a holiday. The house has been completely destroyed by the British. My uncle and others were imprisoned for a long time. Young men were hanged because an important official was killed in an ambush. Whoever had a gun in our city was imprisoned. One old man, over seventy, was hanged because he refused to give his gun away."

A girl of fifteen, who came the following year, related the story of her family's servant:

Sadek was a mason. He boasted of having built houses in Haifa and Jerusalem. He was nearly fifty and upright, with a broad smile on his face. But now Sadek is stooped. He was tortured and blinded by the enemy because he did not tell about his companions, who had vowed to protect their village, Kalkilia. One night the enemy caught some of them. They were tortured. Many never came back. Sadek was old; they were satisfied that he was blinded and helpless. My father keeps him around just to help his family. But Sadek is a miserable old man, and his smile is gone.

Palestinian children in our school found warmth, security, and friends, whose experience in the Arab world across the years was quite disparate.

Wealthy Syrian families had long sent some of their children to us. Suha, whose mother was Turkish and whose father, a diplomat, was the son of an ex-president of the Syrian Republic, came to us when she was twelve. During her last year at school, her father was arrested as a result of a military coup. He and a group of Syrian politicians served long sentences before being exiled to Egypt.

A wealthy landowner from Hama sent us four of his ten children. His eldest daughter, a gentle girl of simple tastes, spent ten years with us. One morning, her father came into my office accompanied by two men, holding a precious purple box. He had come from the jeweler's shop, and he wanted the girl to try on his gift during the morning break. It was a superb gold necklace with diamonds. The girl did not seem at all interested, and though it was a marvel to look upon, I felt uneasy at the sight of glittering gold on the neck of this girl. At school we were trying to acquaint her with a different set of values. A short while after this incident, the family's underpaid driver pleaded with the girl to ask her father to give him a better salary. Much of the family's wealth evaporated when the Syrian government nationalized property in the 1960s.

Before that time, several children from Aleppo, whose families belonged to the landowning class, were used to having servants attend to their slightest needs. Boarding school gave them and other wealthy children, such as those from old Christian families of the Jazira, a sense of discipline. Many became motivated to pursue their higher studies and to prepare themselves for careers. In all this there was a great departure from olden times.

Many girls from conservative families continued to observe traditional customs in the early 1930s, at least some of the time. Azizi, a merry and mischievous girl from an old Damascus family, wore the uniform, a dark blue pleated skirt and white blouse, and appeared as other girls in class, but when the boarders went on a picnic, she put on the black head covering and veiled her face. As soon as we began our mountain climb, though, off came the outer skirt and veil, and Azizi, in her uniform and tennis shoes, climbed as freely as the rest. Many day pupils as well arrived in the morning properly veiled, then laid the coverings aside until it was time to go home. Today, these formalities, for the young people at least, have been set aside.

Although never as numerous as the Syrians, Iraqi children of ambassadors, doctors, engineers, and politicians started coming in appreciable numbers after World War II. Some of their parents were living in Lebanon because of political posts or upheavals. On the whole, they had money, and the children were extravagant and demanding. Many of them identified with Western culture to such an extent that they never spoke their mother tongue. Of course, there were exceptions. Among our students was a girl who became one of the first women in Iraq to take up a diplomatic job. The first pupils we had from Iraq, in fact, were three charming girls whose home breeding had the breath of a liberal atmosphere but the values of a conservative society. Their father, the Iraqi ambassador to Lebanon, accompanied them to school each morning and took coffee with me, speaking with humor and depth of world politics. Like many Arabs, he felt that the United Nations would use its growing influence to solve the Palestinian problem.

The last group of Iraqis, who came in the mid-1960s, were refined and considerate. Many of their parents had studied abroad but had strong feelings about returning to Iraq. Their country was moving into a period of financial prosperity, and they were finding their roots again, taking pride in the opportunities that oil and mineral resources provided for expanding industry. Most of our Jewish Iraqi students would eventually head to Italy; some would go to Hong Kong. None I knew went to Palestine.

The Saudi students also started coming after the war. The first lot of five girls was disappointing, having a great deal of extravagance and no interest in intellectual pursuits. The same was true of the Kuwaitis, whose wealth spoiled their curiosity. Saudis and Kuwaitis of Palestinian parents were more attractive. Many had begun their schooling in Egypt, and on the whole they were very motivated. They labeled themselves revolutionary and progressive. Many went to university for further training. The most remarkable of the Saudi girls was a gentle young woman of eighteen named Thoraya. Her Arabic was advanced thanks to private tutoring, and she wrote exquisite, gemlike lyrics describing the Lebanese landscape.

An interesting bunch of Yemeni students arrived in the late 1960s. Their mothers stayed in Beirut and seemed capable of solving their children's problems with beautiful calm. This was the day of the miniskirt, but these intelligent conservative girls wore their dresses to the ankle and veiled their heads with no apparent word of complaint. Their mothers accompanied them everywhere. All this in the tempestuous atmosphere of Beirut!

After the Suez War of 1956, Egyptian families who came to settle in Lebanon began sending their girls. They usually spoke both French and English but knew almost no Arabic, so it took them time and effort to adjust to our program. Upper-class Egyptians tended to live apart from the ordinary folks and associated only with one another. As Gamal Abdel Nasser Arabized the country, they became ill at ease with themselves and felt further estranged from the life of the community.

Our Lebanese students, who always formed the majority of pupils, were examples for the others. At the start, the girls came mainly from the comfortable middle class, but then we began encouraging intelligent and ambitious children from the poorer classes to enroll. The mixture proved to be extremely healthy. Across the years, our well-to-do girls shed their snobbery and mingled freely with those who were financially less fortunate but usually far more alert and dedicated.

As the day students came from all levels, their political views reflected the unhappy muddle of cold war times. When the big issues came to the fore, there was a veneer of unity among them, which, though thin, managed to withstand the strains of our restless days. The greatest issue on the Lebanese scene was whether Lebanon was an Arab country. The second was whether the Palestinian tragedy was our concern. I was clear in my mind that Lebanon was Arab and that the Palestinian tragedy was of primary concern to us. I felt I shared the opinion of the majority.

XX

IN THE FALL OF 1952, we shifted our home from Beirut to the old family country house in Brummana. The three boys were ready to enter the Quaker School there, while our daughter, Mariam, then ten, became a boarder at the Ahliah School.

Mountain life had a great deal of charm for us. We felt the changing seasons with more intensity, and our children grew to know nature in all its shades. They enjoyed its autumn colors and the luster of the snowy peaks as winter approached. In spring they studied wildflowers and insects; they climbed trees in search of unripe fruit; they examined the little plants as they peeped from their winter shelters. Above all, they befriended village people.

Unlike the city, the village had few social barriers or limitations. Asa'd, who occasionally took care of our garden, was nearly seventy and had been a school worker for more than thirty years, rearing seven children. He wore a faded hat bequeathed to him twenty years earlier by a brother who lived in the States. Asa'd treated the plants with cautious care and joyfully took orders from Mother Cortas, who had once been his boss at Brummana High School. Um Michel walked from a nearby village to serve in our home. The trip up the hills took more than an hour, but although she was around fifty she did it every morning, summer or winter, with vitality. Um Michel had lost her husband in the first world war. She toiled many years in many homes to support her six children. Her pretty daughters married and continued to labor hard. Her two youngest sons became skilled masons, chiseling stones for the new buildings in Brummana. One day the youngest lost his sight from a tumor. His death was sudden.

Our two housemaids, Rahme' and Jameeli, were devoted sisters. They had been orphaned in the first war, and my parents had made them part of the household when they were young. The eldest moved from one relative to another until returning to help me when our third child was born. Her sister was more constant and faithful to us and to her job. She loved perfection and put her heart in her work. She was priceless when the children were babies. She had a talent for winning their love and admiration as no one else could. When she married a man twenty years her junior, she bestowed on him heaps of affection that he did not deserve. With the submissiveness of a crushed female, she worked night and day, obeying a husband who made use of her for his selfish motives. Like millions of others in our part of the world, she believed it's a man's world; the woman's role demanded servitude. Had she been born in an enlightened culture, she might have shown signs of rebellion. For all that, she was an idol to many in the young generation of our family.

Salimi the cook is still with us as I write. Nearly eighty years old, white-haired, toothless, and deaf, with a twinkle in her eye, she does not seem to have changed much in twenty years. With an alert mind, questioning everything and everybody around her and interested in up-to-date gadgets and information, she has a rare, timeless quality. Our grandchild Wadie, Mariam's son, once asked, "Was Salimi ever young?" Indeed, she is an old soul. She remembers how she walked a whole day to get a few kilos of flour during the first war. She remembers the starvation and misery that beset the country when the Turks ruled the East. She coined her own Arabic words for twentieth-century inventions like the radio, the telephone, the airplane, and the elevator. She has an imaginative geography that includes England, France, America, and Africa, but in a profound sense the world for her does not extend beyond Iraq. One thing we could never successfully explain to her was that man had reached the moon!

Beyond the home we came to know Youssef, considered the best barber in town and loved by all the village people for his willingness to help anyone at any time. Once, he left a customer half-shaved in order to lend a hand after a car accident. Another time he left his customer because a little girl asked him to help find her lost dog. Youssef worked with the British army during the war and was proud of his connections, but he was a humanist and opposed war. An officer once surprised him by demanding his arrest. "What for?" Youssef asked.

"You killed a grand old serpent."

"This I did to save others."

"The serpent was not harmful," the officer said, "and you must be kind to animals."

"Every day you and your colleagues kill innocent young men," Youssef burst out. "Why don't you preach kindness to mankind?"

After the exodus of 1948 a number of Palestinian families took refuge in Brummana's calm. Most of them were perplexed, having left their land and property, flying from danger, keen with hopes of return and utterly without assurance that those hopes could be realized. The bootblack, a gentle elderly man, came from Acre. He had been a mason and boasted of helping to build large structures in Damascus, Haifa, Jerusalem, and Baghdad. When he was forced to leave Palestine, the only job available to him was shining shoes. As the years groaned on, many children of these Palestinian refugees migrated to Canada or Australia.

A number of Europeans and British also made Brummana their home. There was a miserable Greek drunkard who landed in the village, possibly from Tiberius. His health was failing, and he walked silently down the streets, friendless, though people would greet him with a word or two. Maurice and his sister, who had originally emigrated from Germany to Haifa, owned a shop that carried all the varieties of foods the children liked. Wega Little had German, Ethiopian, and British blood in her veins and ran a hotel with a cosmopolitan atmosphere. Mrs. Little shared many a story with Mother Cortas of the famine that had devastated the area in the first world war, of the defeated Turkish soldiers who fled in the face of the British, and of the Allied armies during the second war. Her daughter, Sylvia, in the prime of her youth, had lost the flavor of living. Often she found solace in a glass of alcohol at the end of an empty day.

In the 1950s Brummana High School, which our boys attended, had 600 students representing more than twenty nationalities. Most of the boarders came from neighboring Arab countries, mainly Syria. On the whole, they were wealthy, and very few had a clear sense of purpose. The day scholars, on the other hand, came from the outlying villages and were usually poor but worked hard to attain respectable grades.

Herbert and Gwen Dobbing headed the school. They were a cultured couple from Britain who won the admiration of the community. Herbert, the headmaster, loved the students and inculcated a passion for classical music. Our boys took delight in drama and in the drama coach, Freddy, who was full of gaiety. Freddy was masterful at reading bits of humorous poetry and prose, and was always applauded joyously.

When school ended and summer arrived, Brummana lost its quiet. Its hotels were packed with holiday-makers from East and West. The highlight of summer was the International Tennis Tournament, which attracted players and fans from all over the world. Bit by bit the village became more sophisticated. Wealthy Lebanese returned from the States and invested money in buildings and hotels. The nightclubs and restaurants became renowned. But with sophistication came an unwelcome materialism, which eclipsed Brummana's modest charm.

Through these changes I increasingly appreciated Mother Cortas, the solid foundation of our happy home and a treasure whom her grandchildren adored. A friend from abroad once said, "I was always impressed by the presence of the very old enjoying the very young in your country. This pattern has disappeared from our lives in the West. The family has been partitioned."

In the East, it was perhaps the only thing that had not been partitioned. For parents like us, with pressing duties, the older generation's wisdom and experience gave our home life order and rhythm. Grandmother took care of the children when we were away. She made it possible for us to invite friends and acquaintances any time and be sure of their receiving a warm welcome. Everything was beautifully arranged by the first lady of our house. Because of her I am sure my children acquired a reverence for the elderly that few Western children have.

Grandmother had a fantastic memory for dates. Old villagers came to ask her the ages of their family members. Not only was she able to recall the day in the year but very often the exact hour of the day of birth. She loved birthdays, and with a large family she regularly had cakes to prepare. Once, in anticipation of a one-day holiday, Ramzi, then six years old, asked his teacher why there would be no school that day. "It is Prophet Muhammad's birthday," the teacher answered. "Do you know who the Prophet is?"

"I don't," he said, "but surely my Grandmother does, and I hope she has a cake for him."

When Grandmother grew older, she would ask our eldest son, Nadim, then about fourteen, to mix the cake batter for her. Her recipe book in hand, she would give special attention to measuring and weighing every ingredient. Ramzi, around twelve, with no interest in cooking, would make fun of his brother, saying, "Here you are, a cook like a woman." Nadim would answer back, "This is not cooking; it is food chemistry." Nadim continued to enjoy his food chemistry through adulthood, taking a break from doctoring to help his wife prepare his grandmother's recipes.

Mother Cortas passed away on December 16, 1967. She had collapsed on the anniversary of her youngest grandchild's birth. "It's Lina's birthday," she said. "Did someone remember to bake her a cake?" And that was all.

XXI

~

I n October 1954, I revisited America. My hosts, the Stokes family, wealthy Quakers who lived in New Jersey, had been known for many generations for their benevolence and commitment to world peace. I was grateful for the opportunity to speak about the Palestinian problem to a group of wealthy Americans as well as to a number of audiences in schools and meetings. Although my words were only a drop in the bucket, perhaps they had a small effect on some of those who wanted to know the truth.

I spoke of Count Bernadotte and of the findings of the United Nations observers after his assassination. In Beirut I had become acquainted with a remarkable member of the team, Cmdr. E. H. Hutchinson. He had come to the Middle East in 1951, convinced that the new Zionist state wanted peace and that Arabs were the only impediment. Several times Arabs had visited with Commander Hutchinson, but it was not our opinions that changed his views. He was searching for facts, and he found many of those to rely upon.

Bernadotte's final report had stated that the greatest obstacle to peace in the region was the predicament of Palestine's refugees. One of the earliest UN reports suggested that the heads of Arab refugee families be interviewed as a step toward returning them to their homes in the demilitarized zone. Many Arabs wished to be interviewed, but few were allowed to meet the observers, and the report concluded that the Israelis rejected the Arabs' right to return to their homes. Meanwhile, border raids continued, and Israel's frontier line, which had not been drawn to respect village boundaries, invited trouble, cutting villages and towns in two and leaving scars in the heart of Jerusalem. Many Arab villages were left without land.

Commander Hutchinson's first major investigation involved an Israeli raid near Bethlehem in January of 1952. Men, women, and children had been gunned down in their homes. Israel was condemned for this act by the Mixed Armistice Commission, but its leaders made no attempt to bring those responsible to trial. This was only one of many Israeli acts carefully documented by the UN observers but never publicized in the Western press.

The worst trouble came when Israeli forces began to carry loads of arms into Jerusalem in preparation for a final conquest of the city. They had already seized the property and homes of well-to-do Arabs and had taken schools and hospitals. Now they were determined to take the small historic area of the Old City. But the Arabs were alerted, and here they held their ground.

In compliance with the UN agreement, the Arabs left the Hebrew University area as an island under UN control. It never occurred to them that this control would eventually be taken over by the Israelis. Each fortnight the Arab forces allowed an Israeli convoy to pass through the Old City carrying provisions to the guards. On more than one occasion the Israelis tried to smuggle in arms and dynamite but were discovered by the UN observers.

I told my American audiences of these things and quoted a number of wise Jews, some of whom had bravely expressed their opposition to a Zionist state before it became a reality. I told them of Albert Einstein, who was formally offered the presidency of Israel after Chaim Weizmann died, in 1952, with a note that he belonged to the Jews and not to Princeton. Einstein, who was deeply interested in the Hebrew University, rejected Jewish nationalism, supported a binational state of Palestine, and condemned violence and terrorism.

"The State idea is not to my heart's liking," he said. "I cannot understand why it is needed. It is connected with narrowmindedness. I should much rather see a reasonable agreement with the Arabs on the basis of living together than a Jewish state in Palestine."

When I spoke at Haverford College outside Philadelphia, students listened intently, but some of their professors seemed content with their own findings. Most of them did not realize that Israel had come into being as a result of many years of aggressive battles. I recognized then that in the United States the Zionists had been most active in influencing intellectual circles and that as a result the American public at large was ignorant of much that had shaped our world.

After taking part in an international conference in Cleveland, I flew to Washington, D.C. The capital was a dream from the air. The autumn foliage brightened its marble monuments. The Potomac River flowed amid gardens aflame with fiery red and yellow leaves. The airport was teeming with people when our plane landed. Coming from the Eastern world overwhelmed with a desire for freedom, I found the Lincoln Memorial to be the most inspiring monument. I lingered there meditating on the inscription on the white tablets. Do American politicians today read these words? I wondered. If they do, why do they hesitate to speak out in the interest of liberty? It is not as if they simply had to take the Arabs' word on the Palestinian situation.

Almost a year later, in December of 1955, the Ihud Association, then an important political organization in Israel, declared:

In the end we must come publicly with the truth. We have no moral right to oppose the return of the refugees to their land. We have no right to ask the American Jews to leave their country to which they are attached, and settle in a land that has been stolen from others, while the owners are homeless and miserable. We have no right to occupy the house of an Arab if we have not paid for it. The same goes for fields, gardens, shops and stores. We have no right to build a settlement on other people's property. To do this is robbery. We are faced with this choice— either to listen to the voice of truth, or not to listen and to bring evil and misfortune upon us and the future generations.

XXII

࿐

"WHAT DOES IT MEAN to be an emperor? To be a farmer is nobler," one of the boarders exclaimed in the midst of an uproar among the girls at school one day. The cause: a royal wedding, the third for the Shah of Iran, this time to the gracious Farah Diba. Radio reports were breathless. Television carried pictures of the new empress's glittering jewels. But whereas in my childhood this would have been cause for excitement among the youngsters, in the late 1950s it was a cause for argument. The Palestinian students were disgusted, the Iranians split, the rest indifferent and therefore of no consequence to the combatants who pressed their case.

History had pivoted. A few years before, on the eve of the Egyptian Revolution of 1952, King Farouk was too insignificant to be bothered with. In my youth the exploits of his ancestors formed a colorful chapter in Arab history. His great-grandfather had freed the country from the Napoleonic expedition. His grandfather Ibrahim Pasha had expanded the empire into Syria, Palestine, and Arabia proper. But young Farouk ascended the throne in 1936, when England was tightening the reins on the colonies. Full of hope, backed by all the

Arab countries, he could have saved the dignity of Arab independence. Instead, he retreated into greed and self-indulgence
and sank to the lowest levels. He gave the British complete control of the Suez Canal, their imperial lifeline to Africa and
India. By the 1950s the young officers, headed by Nasser, just
wanted the king out of the way. When Farouk agreed to abdi-
cate, the Egyptians exhaled in joyful relief. He died in 1966, an
ignominious end.

To Arab youth, Nasser was the new man. He instilled a sense
of pride and symbolized the militant anticolonial spirit of the
time. One morning in March of 1955, I came to school to discover that our students were on strike. They were protesting the
Baghdad Pact, a cold war security alliance with Britain that had
been advocated throughout the Arab world by Nuri as-Said, the
powerful prime minister of Iraq.[1] To Iraq, Britain was indispensable, and Nuri had been shuttling between Iraq and Egypt for
months trying to convince Egypt's leaders of the advantages of
formally siding with the West. But Nasser and his colleagues had
grievous memories of Western double-dealing and saw no wisdom in signing another pact. "Over seventy times Britain has
broken her promise to evacuate the canal," they said. Although
the Italians had been driven from Libya by the Allies, the British
had plans to stay. The French insisted on keeping bases in
Tunisia. They maintained ruthless control over Algeria, which
was in revolt. They had ousted the Sultan of Morocco and replaced him with a lackey.

In Egypt, the young officers advocated a stance of nonalignment. The Iraqi and Egyptian leaders met at Sarsand, in the
Iraqi mountains, but came to no better understanding. Nasser
wished to present a unified, independent Arab front to the West
as the only possible way out of servitude. That was unthinkable

to Iraq. Nuri decided to ignore Egypt and create a pro-Western
front with other Middle Eastern countries, confident that the
young Arab countries would follow. Turkey, Iran, and Pakistan
were invited to sign the pact. No sooner was it signed than dis-
sent shook the Arab world. Our students' strike was part of that.
Demonstrations and parades filled our public squares. Young
people lined the streets, shouting slogans against the West. The
young revolutionary group in Egypt had won the support of the
new generation.

Outside the Arab world the idea of nonalignment was gaining strength. In the city of Bandung, Indonesia, representatives
from nine Arab states and twenty Asiatic and African states
met later that year to discuss the problem of colonialism and
the necessity of mutual support among newly independent
states. The Arab leaders, headed by Nasser, won a symbolic
victory for Palestine. The Bandung Conference insisted that
the relevant UN resolutions be implemented. Israel's defiance
of those resolutions had not abated. Prime Minister David
Ben-Gurion had moved his government seat to Jerusalem in
1949, and by the 1950s all the Israeli ministries were there. Not
one powerful country condemned this illegal act. Dag Ham-
marskjöld did, after becoming UN Secretary General in 1953,
but he was alone.

It is difficult to overstate the depth of the uneasiness that
small countries felt in those cold war years. The UN had been
established to abolish war, yet there was war. NATO was the
mightiest military alliance in history, capable of dealing a blow
that could wipe out a large portion of the human race, yet most
of the world's people were powerless to control it. I remember
listening to a radio program in 1956 celebrating the seventh
birthday of NATO. My son Sami, who was nine, was listening
with me. Details of the broadcast were of no interest to him. He

just wanted to know, "If war breaks out, who will be with us and who will be against us?"

"What war?" I said. "There is no war. The war is over, and you need not worry about these things. No one is against us."

"Are you by any chance deaf, Mummy?" he said. "Or are you making yourself stupid today?" I was sad realizing that this child of nine was aware of the terrible threat hanging over the world.

At the same time, as I recall those years, it would be a mistake to understate the sense of confidence we in the Arab world felt because of Nasser. An Egyptian correspondent put it to us better than anyone:

Nobody can ever forget that Nasser nationalized the canal; and nobody outside Egypt can ever understand what that means to Egyptians. They [the British and French] took thousands of Egyptians out of the villages under the whip and made them dig the canal. Fifty thousand Egyptians died and then, bit by bit, they stole the whole thing from us. You can never understand what Nasser came to mean because he got the canal back for us. In spite of his mistakes, and certainly they were many, Nasser awakened in us a sense of self-respect and dignity that no Arab ruler had.

It was on July 26, 1956, when, from the city of Alexandria, Nasser announced, "The Suez Canal was built by Egyptians; it belongs to Egypt." My husband, my brother-in-law, and I were driving to Beirut when we heard the startling news over the radio. Both men were alarmed. "What foolishness!" one of them said. "How can we defy the West?" It was a frightening venture. They were businessmen, and like most in Lebanese business circles, they worried about nothing so much as unpredictability. Iran's experiment in nationalization under Mohammad Mossadegh was also fresh in their minds. Did Nasser not see what had happened there? Mossadegh nationalized the oil industry in 1951. Britain blockaded the country and plunged it into economic crisis; by 1953 Mossadegh had been ousted in a coup, and reform was finished. "Why does Nasser risk the future of Egypt to satisfy his ambition?" they asked.

With that tone, part of the Lebanese press criticized the daring act. Through the summer my husband's business in Lebanon, like all local enterprises, suffered setbacks. But people were irresistibly fascinated by Nasser's position. In the ensuing months traffic through the canal continued as normal. Every twenty-four hours nearly fifty ships were piloted through the waters, paying the usual fee. When a number of European pilots refused to cooperate, Egyptian and Greek pilots took over the task. In Lebanon the tone started changing, as the public cheered Nasser's act. "For once, we have a leader who is not afraid to stand up to our enemies," people said.

The Palestinian tragedy had confirmed their belief in an untrustworthy Europe. When the World Bank canceled its commitment to finance the Aswan High Dam because Egypt had recognized China and bought arms from the Soviet bloc, people felt that the world community was intent on humiliating Egypt. Nasser said he was nationalizing the canal to finance the dam, and with that assertion he proved his independence of the West. As he would say, "We have to defend our rights to the last drop of our blood."

The radio broadcast his speeches assuring that indemnities would be paid to the canal's shareholders. No incidents against foreigners occurred in the Egyptian cities. Everybody was treated with courtesy. The average man in the street was aware only of pride in a powerful leader.[2] But in autumn all the European pilots except the Greeks left the canal area. In late October the Israelis invaded Gaza and the Sinai. Within days Britain and France invaded the canal area. It was a short war, brought to a halt by U.S. President Eisenhower and action by the UN. The British and French were forced to withdraw by year's end; the Israelis, a few months later.

Many Arabs still think of Eisenhower as the bravest American president. His words in a report to the nation will always remain of great value:

> There can be no peace without law, and there can be no law if
> we are to invoke one code of international conduct for those
> who oppose us and another for our friends. We judge no man by
> his name or inheritance but by what he does and for what he
> stands, and so likewise we judge other nations.

Yet after the war Britain boycotted Egypt, and the country's assets in Western banks were frozen. The canal was inoperable because of war wreckage, so income dried up. In January 1957, the press reported that Nasser had appealed to U.S. Secretary of State John Foster Dulles for emergency assistance for wheat, penicillin, and petrol, of which Egypt had hardly a week's stock. Dulles refused. Nasser made a second appeal to Washington, for the release of some of Egypt's frozen dollars to enable him to purchase drugs for the hospitals. That too was refused. So Nasser turned to Russia. Immediately wheat and medicines were supplied in abundance. This news was brought to my attention by a person who judged me to be an admirer of Eisenhower. When the facts were verified, they put all of us who trusted America to shame.

We had imagined America as a savior. It wasn't. It had intervened in Suez for its own reasons. After the war, Europe was finished as an imperial power. It would take years before all the colonies achieved independence, but Britain and France would never again dominate our world as they had. There was a new power now, and I had to remind myself of what my father had said some thirty years before: "No one loves us because of our black eyes."

XXIII

~

Fragments from a Shattered Place

1957

The smell of the red earth in the Bekaa Valley was fresh with
the dews of April. Thin clouds sailed across a superb blue sky.
Our old Ford was traveling down the new road to Palestine,
which avoided occupied territory. Our children's excitement was
high. This was their first crossing to Syria and Palestine. They
knew the Holy Land from Bible stories; soon they would see it.
At the gates of Damascus, the fragrance of blooming orchards
filled the air, but we had no time to stop and passed into the
green wheat fields of Huran. Herds of cattle were moving along
the open road; in the distance, strings of camels.

The coastal route to Jerusalem, used through the centuries
by the Phoenicians and the Romans, Byzantines and Arabs, was
now cut off. Our children would never travel the historic pilgrim road of their great-grandfathers. Theirs and ours now was
a longer road that went winding through the barrens of Transjordan. Our youngest son, Sami, gazing out the window, re-
marked, "I never thought shepherds carried rifles."

Roads told the new story of division. As we approached the Holy City, an exhausted policeman whistled us back from the route we were about to take. "Don't go that way! It is the old road; it cuts through enemy territory!"

The route from Bethlehem to Jerusalem was no longer a short trip but required a lengthy detour. If shepherds on the nearby hills heard the angels' song today, they would have a long trudge to the manger.

All roads to the Hebrew University, a Jewish enclave on a hill facing the Lutheran Augusta Victoria Hospital, crossed through Arab Jerusalem.

Easter morning. In Jerusalem thousands of pilgrims, following an ancient tradition, had prayed through the night, waiting for the Resurrection. At daybreak, when their Christ was risen, they dispersed with words of mercy in their hearts. Church bells chimed. The clear sound of the muezzin's call to prayer echoed in the streets. This was the real and eternal Jerusalem that Caliph Omar had invoked in the seventh century. And yet it was a mirage.

We left the Holy City in the early hours and drove through the scorching heat toward Jericho. Along the austere hills twisted the road that the Good Samaritan had traveled, carrying to safety the poor man who had fallen into the hands of robbers. We approached the Dead Sea, crystal blue. The children enjoyed floating in the salty water. I looked across to the cliffs of Moab and along the lonely hills, where once the Essenes had lived recording their precious scrolls, where Herod had his winter palace surrounded by a palm garden, where Omay princes had come for hunting and sports.

We drove on, to the middle of a dry valley where Musa Alami, a wealthy independent gentleman, had built an oasis. He had been determined to do something for the young people adrift after the Zionists had scattered the Palestinians from their homes. Year after year, through the harshest seasons, he and his men had dug into the dry earth in search of water. And then one morning water gushed from the depths. Now Alami had hundreds of lost or orphaned boys to bring forth the soil's wealth. Young men whose parents had left their orange groves in Haifa or Jaffa labored on the land with the hope of better days. Boys whose fathers had worked the soil in land now lost to them learned to farm. They called Alami "the man who brought the water to the desert."

Palestinian agriculture had been stricken since 1948. This is what happened in Battir, an ancient town situated in the hills around Jerusalem and overlooking a fertile valley. Battir had long been the last train stop between Lydda and Cairo. A fountain bubbled in the heart of the village. Springs flowing from the mountains irrigated the valleys, and fruits and vegetables from here filled the markets of Jerusalem. This happy picture changed after the demarcation of a frontier. Train service to Cairo stopped. Half of the fertile land was now declared part of Israel, and the road between Battir and Jerusalem was cut. The nearest town was Bethlehem. Thousands of people were marooned. When no peace settlement occurred, a new route linking the village again with Jerusalem had to be found. A team of men worked doggedly to lay the road. When it was completed there was a glow of achievement, the joy of a collective enterprise, among the people.

The problem of Palestine was not contained within frontiers. How could it be? After the Suez War the British writer Michael Adams observed, "Those refugees in their stone hillsides and in desolate valleys on sandy wastes about Gaza, and in hovels on the glittering fringes of Beirut, are a million witnesses to the fact that Britain failed in something she had set her hand to do. As a result of this failure, the state of Israel came into being. The Arabs were never given a guarantee against the continuous expansion of Israel.". The fate of the refugees shaped our fate in Lebanon. And time after time the Zionists invaded our southern region. Borders mattered now, and our small army had no real control of ours.

1958

The wise voices in our press gave approval to Arab unity in whatever form it took. It made sense that Egypt and Syria would declare an alliance. A large sector of the public even approved when Jordan chose to unite with Iraq in the Baghdad Pact. Unfortunately, the intrigues of the cold war swayed us back and forth. At one time we were afraid of Russia; at another, of the United States. The farsighted among us felt the danger of being exploited by either side.

Lebanon was boiling internally, as different factions sought their own advantage. From May to September, Lebanon experienced the cruelties of civil war. When a new president, Gen. Fouad Chehab, took over, animosities seemed to dwindle. People started to patch up their differences. The most severe were pushed into the background. For a while, a long brutal war was deferred.

Iraq was on fire in July of 1958. King Faisal II and his family were killed. Most of the men in power and a considerable number of notables fled the country. Nuri as-Said, caught fleeing in women's clothes, was brutally slain; then his body was dragged through the city. The coup, led by Gen. Abdul Karim Qasim, was savage. Many of us, remembering the example of Egypt, thought that Iraq could have got rid of its monarchy by less bloody measures. The stories that filled our press were unbelievably cruel. For a while we were completely cut off from Iraq. General Qasim withdrew Iraq from the Baghdad Pact, which had to be renamed.

1959

Five years since the Algerian Revolution began. Three years since the Battle of Algiers—the general strike, the bombings, the tortures. Two years since the forced transfer of two million Algerians from the countryside into French concentration camps, their cropland, their orchards, ruined. The National Liberation Front exhibited feats of heroism that history will record with admiration. Hardly 30,000 freedom fighters confronted the tanks and heavy arms of nearly half a million French soldiers. De Gaulle was president of France. For all his difficulties at home, he was becoming very popular in the Arab world. We watched and waited. It would be three more years before Algeria was freed from French colonialism.

1960

Political disaster had weakened our faith in human cooperation; national disaster would revive a slim sense of hope. In February an earthquake completely destroyed the Moroccan city of Agadir. Twelve thousand people were estimated missing or dead. A world relief movement arose. Naval fleets from many countries headed toward the Mediterranean port. Aircraft, particularly American helicopters, rescued the injured and homeless. Strong nations, we saw, were capable of doing something besides foment trouble. Humanity could still be awakened.

XXIV

❦

IN THE 1960s enrollment at our school expanded by a marked degree. Our students came not only from Lebanon and the Middle East but from the African colonies, where some Lebanese families lived. The students' economic, social, and racial backgrounds were also increasingly varied. I felt it my duty to try to meet the needs of the greatest number possible with resourcefulness and an open mind. Not all on my staff saw eye to eye with me on the value of such diversity. I had to cope with some unpleasant situations trying to persuade my colleagues of the significant internationalist role we were called upon to play. Luckily, they ultimately all cooperated in the finest spirit possible.

At this particular period, education in the Arab countries was uneven. Lebanon had had a national school for girls since 1916, for instance, while Algeria was just beginning to broaden and Arabize education in 1964.[1] A difference in the cultural and economic backgrounds of the pupils created gaps in understanding and ability. The diversity of foreign schools in Lebanon intensified those differences. My main concern at the start was to teach the most intelligent students. If that came at the expense of the wealthy, so be it.

Time has dimmed some marvelous memories of the many extremely bright girls who trusted us when we discovered their intellectual potential and hidden talents. But I look back with a general happiness that we gave a chance to so many who otherwise would have had no means of getting one, and that the school as a whole was stimulated by the circulation of so much new blood.

Although political upheavals constantly shook our area, all of our students found an atmosphere conducive to preparation for a purposeful life. To me a school was primarily a human institution, and a human approach took precedence over all other considerations. For that reason also I was determined to expose our girls to the insights and experiences of remarkable individuals from all over the world. In 1960 we heard Nehru, whose public lecture was so crowded that hundreds of people sat outside under the trees listening via loudspeaker as he stressed that noble ends cannot be attained by ignoble means. Over the years, our school assemblies welcomed such varied figures as Horace Alexander, an English humanitarian writer who had joined Gandhi's ashram; Dorothy Thompson, an American journalist; Bertha Vester, a grand old lady from Jerusalem whose family had founded the American Colony and who herself had established a children's hospital and welfare center; Madame Labouisse, whose husband directed the UN Relief and Welfare Agency (UNRWA) in Lebanon and who was the daughter of Marie Curie; Vijaya Lakshmi Pandit, who was Nehru's sister and the first woman president of the UN General Assembly; Helen Keller, who told the girls her only unhappiness came "when I think of the inevitable suffering of mankind"; a Burmese scholar, who spoke on the rights of the child; a lady doctor who'd worked thirty-five years in China and prompted a heated discussion by saying that "Asia was not pro-East or pro-West but pro-bread," and that when the problem of starvation was solved, we could then talk about human rights.

These guests and others helped our girls stretch their imaginative and critical faculties. Some made us realize that our problems were only a drop compared with the world's problems. Still, the ember burns where it falls, goes an Arab proverb. We could not spare our girls from being upset about the troubles in our area, but we could arm them with perspective and a scale of values that would always serve them.

It gives me immense satisfaction to realize that after forty years of trial, the experiment proved to be worthwhile. Our students left us with a sounder knowledge of the Arab world's problems and a sincere appreciation of what we had given them. Nationalism as a chauvinistic ideal never took root in our school. Fairness, humanity, and principles of equal rights to all found deep expression in our collective inner life.

It was, however, a tumultuous experience. Living with the reality of the atomic bomb and the West's blind support of Israel under all circumstances could easily undercut our message of universal brotherhood. The UN's activities nourished us with optimism for a brighter future. At the same time, the world was insecure, and in the early 1960s our youth were rebellious. Sometimes their cynicism overpowered us. When U.S. President John Kennedy initiated the Peace Corps, calling on the youth of America to help the underdeveloped world, our girls were not impressed. I invited an attractive young American to speak about this project, which reached fifty countries of Africa, Asia, and South America, but her words did not mean much to some of our youngsters. "Stopping arms deals is the surest way of establishing peace," cried one of our girls to this woman, who could not really be blamed for what was happening in the world at large. In the summer of 1963, when the black people of America marched on Washington for equity and a fair deal, some of our girls questioned the wisdom of the act, considering it to be merely theatrical. A decade of mistrust and violence was being ushered onto our doorsteps. Our school aimed to instill a passion for cooperation and justice, but deplorable events all over the world had weakened the youth's faith in Western civilization. Struggles in Africa and the Middle East captured their imaginations and inflamed their rebellious spirit. It was not always easy for us to balance realism and the idea of genuine human solidarity.

The makeup of our school helped here, even as it reflected the world's competing forces. More and more children whose parents were working with UNICEF, the Food and Agriculture Organization, and UNESCO came to us. As the years passed, our international representation broadened. We had Americans, British, Indians, Pakistanis, Norwegians, Japanese, Portuguese from Mozambique, South Africans of Dutch origin, Ghanaians, Ugandans, Iranians, Greeks and Cypriots, Germans, Hungarians, Russians, and Turks. All of these students fit admirably into the school pattern, creating a cosmopolitan atmosphere where cooperation and trust overpowered narrow nationalism.

Our Arab community expanded, too, to include students from Kuwait, Egypt, Yemen, and the Gulf area, as well as Lebanese who had made homes in Ecuador, Ghana, Nigeria, Mali, Somaliland, Libya, Morocco, Sudan, Trinidad, and Jamaica. In many instances these children were the first generation in their families to have regular schooling. In this ever-widening world of young girls and boys, I found inspiration and joy. The more the geographic boundary expanded, the happier I felt.

In 1960 my staff and school friends arranged a twenty-fifth-anniversary celebration of my work at Ahliah. The girls put on a play they had written about our school life. They called it *A Visitor from Mars*. In it, my character received a prince and his daughter who had had to leave their planet, Mars, due to a political upheaval. The other students went on strike and refused to accept the newcomer, who looked peculiar and had strange ways. But when the school committee objected, the girls had a change of heart, took up my side, and opened their arms to welcome the newcomer.

Indeed, we had no strangers in our midst. The more we lived together, the more we discovered the sublime human bonds that linked us. At all times and in all circumstances, the realm in which we shared was always vaster than the realm in which we differed. The truth of that was typified in the great number of mixed marriages I came to see in the families of our students. I discovered to my great joy that these mixed marriages gave a new rhythm to our lives. Perhaps they also enhanced the intelligence of our students on the whole. There is no doubt in my mind that mixed marriages, when successful, bring out the best in human nature. Love expands its horizon and embraces new cultural vistas and modes of living. Apprehension gives way to trust, and trust to affection.

In my experience, I have come across two types of mixed marriages. One I would label moderately risky. It involves people of similar cultural orbits, like Greeks and Italians, Egyptians and Sudanese, Germans and French, Indonesians and Dutch, Americans and British. Usually people from geographic areas that adopt the same cultural patterns find the differences of daily living less disturbing.

The marriages that I usually label risky involve people from environments with modes of living unfamiliar to each other, like Greeks and Americans, Turks and French, Russians and Italians, Spaniards and Scandinavians. Still, I must admit that a happy marriage is the product of the human character. If two people's values are in harmony, marriage has a good chance of survival. Most mixed marriages I have come across illustrate that the sacred institution of the family has a great chance of survival. Invariably, the children cling to the family bond and help give marriage durability and depth. The world has not yet discovered any substitute for family happiness.

XXV

❧

•

"O**UR SWEETEST SONGS** are those that tell of saddest thoughts," wrote the poet Shelley. This was true of the Palestinian songs that were written after the war of 1948. They were full of melancholy. War was not the answer to the Palestinian plight. Love of the earth, the blessings of its abundance, and a firm belief in ultimate justice kept ablaze the hope of return. Even the youth, who secretly dreamed of revenge, shared in this rich heritage of poetry and song, which elevated longing and the land.

Beginning in the 1950s, as the Israelis continued acts of violence in the quiet countryside, village songs acquired a certain defiance. By the late 1950s a new type of song was born throughout the world. As it reached our youth, the pastoral, nostalgic Palestinian melodies disappeared. By the late 1960s they had been replaced by a militant anger:

Now that I have a gun, Palestine has become so near
It is only a few steps away
My gun will surely take me back home
Only my gun can get back the land.

The advent of a new era for Palestine appeared as a mere speck on the horizon on January 1, 1965. A small news item in an obscure corner of our daily papers noted that a band of commandos had undertaken a successful operation in occupied Palestine. The words were brief but to the point. Those of us interested in the cause noticed and inquired, but there was much skepticism. Who are these young men? How strong are they? Will this be the beginning and the end? We had seen so much of failure. We were afraid to hope.

Each day the news became clearer. The Israelis were alarmed, but to us the news of these young men was fresh as springwater. Faith in the homeland: Was this not the cry of thousands of young people living in the camps? Was this not their dream— repatriation and return? More hope filled our hearts as our freedom fighters crossed the wires and aroused fear among the aggressors. For me, it was the hope that the aggression would stop, that resistance would command the world's attention and force a just solution to the Palestinian crisis. International assessments of the scope of the commando activities varied, but one thing was sure: the display of force attracted the world's notice far more than had all the legal arguments of the Arab League.

I was lucky to visit Palestine during that period for a regional conference in Jerusalem. During a brief stay, I renewed old friendships and observed the tremendous growth of the Old City. Arab Jerusalem was alive with tourists. Hotels and buildings were rising everywhere, their rosy stones sparkling in the midday sun. The hills around the city and on the way to Ramallah were teeming with vitality. There was no evidence of a military presence. In its dignity, Jerusalem reminded me of the good old days. There were more schools and hospitals, more welfare centers. No one can stop the strength of a determined people, I thought. A great deal of credit was given to the farsighted mayor of the city, Ruhi Khatib. He had taken it upon himself to see that his dear birthplace enjoyed healthy expansion along the neighboring hills without spoiling its historic beauty. It had been almost ten years since I had last seen it, and still no city in the world could rival Jerusalem for its charm and mystery.

Late in the afternoon a friend drove me down the Dead Sea road en route home. The sun was setting behind us. The golden sands stretched for miles until we reached the oasis of Jericho. In the distance, I could see the trees of Musa Alami's Agricultural Colony. It was prosperous now. When we crossed into Jordan, Amman was bursting with life. New villas were dispersed on the hills, landscaped with flowerbeds that gave bursts of color to the arid surroundings. The Royal Palace was a picture of beauty and harmony. But Amman also had its miserable camps, where thousands of uprooted Palestinians lived in deplorable habitations and despair. UNRWA continued to bring food and medicine and to educate as many as possible, but who wants to live on charity all his life? The babies were growing into childhood, the youth into adulthood; the aged were dying out. "Wait and see," one young man told us. "Someday we will fight our way back."

This is what all the youth were saying: those I met in Amman, in Damascus, and in Beirut. They all wanted to fight their way back, across the barbed wires, across the land mines and dynamite, across all the dangers. "Peace got us nowhere," they said. "Let us try war." This tone echoed through their speech and song. It seemed also to echo through the hills. Nothing could stop it.

The young men continued their secret training. Many of the older generation remained complacent. "Our cause is plain as the sun and will surely win in the end" was their attitude. They did not stop to think that a friendless justice does not interest humanity. We all knew the Arab proverb "No right is lost if it has a defender." Although in the end justice may prevail, justice has to be defended lest it be lost in the labyrinth of human scheming. The Israeli army, meanwhile, had formed a special unit to mount raids on border villages. Two years passed. The commando actions persisted, but when war came, it was not so much because of them as despite them.

May 1967 was mild and beautiful in Beirut. Our eldest son, Nadim, was due to take his medical degree in June. The American University was planning a centennial celebration for its graduates. Our son had invited a young Scottish doctor to stay with us for a fortnight, and although there was great tension on the borders, the two decided to drive to Jerusalem because the Scotsman had never seen Palestine. They took a leisurely trip. On May 23 the young doctors were in Sidon lending a hand at a hospital when they heard that Nasser had declared the closing of the Straits of Tiran at Sharm el-Sheikh. Rumors of an Israeli military mobilization were rife.[1]

On May 24, I had an American gentleman scheduled to speak at the school, but I had to cancel the meeting. It disturbed me immensely, as this man had worked in the youth camps and had great sympathy for the Arab cause. But his country was openly helping the enemy. Our girls were extremely agitated, and even the word "American" set them off.

When UN Secretary General U Thant traveled to Egypt, we hoped that the tension would lessen. Then the Soviet Union declared its willingness to support the Arabs in case of war. We had an Arab speaker at an assembly who brought a large map and spoke of Aqaba and the Red Sea port. He explained how insignificant Sharm el-Sheikh was both commercially and strategically to Israel and seemed pretty sure that the Zionists would not start a war for it.[2] "Israel," he said, "thrives on expansion, but this time it won't be as easy as before."

By May 29 the press all over Europe was following the tension in occupied Palestine. At school the girls prepared a debate on oil and its importance in liberating the country. There was a great difference of opinion, but the discussion was enlightening. Arab solidarity seemed to intensify. At the demand of Egypt, the UN Security Council met on May 30. A day later, Jordan's King Hussein flew to meet Nasser. At school we had visits from the Red Cross, whose representatives attempted to teach the girls first aid, but there was not much preplanning and the students were too disturbed to relax and learn.

On June 2 the American University's students staged a silent strike. Soon U.S. and British citizens began leaving Lebanon. Some were our friends and felt ill at ease about their country's policies, but few came to say goodbye. On Monday, June 5, we were carrying on a normal school day when a father rushed in to take his two daughters home. It was 10 a.m. We had not yet heard that the Israeli troops were attacking the Sinai. With every minute, another parent rang the school bell. There was nothing to do but to dismiss classes. The whole country was roiled. We had no idea what might happen.

That first day the military situation in the Sinai was greatly confused. We heard that Jordan was being attacked through the Jerusalem sector. Syria was advancing from the north. Rumors spread that the Israelis had completely overtaken the Gaza Strip. Jerusalem was in a terrible state. The American University hospital received a Telex from there asking for medical aid; a group of twenty-two Arab doctors, including Nadim, left at once. We were extremely worried about them; the Israelis were shelling Jerusalem heavily. Before the doctors could reach it, the Holy City surrendered, on June 7. The doctors were stationed in Az Zarqa, Jordan, where they treated hundreds of napalm cases. The Israelis had achieved a military victory beyond anyone's expectations, and they reveled in it.

Immediately after, a group of concerned individuals in Lebanon formed an association called the Friends of Jerusalem, with the sole objective of helping the people in the occupied territories resist aggression. It was the idea of Dr. Najib Abu-Haidar of the American University and his wife, Nancy, who were in Jerusalem when the city was seized. Nancy, an American, wrote a moving open letter appealing to her countrymen to understand the situation. Half a million copies of this document reached people across the world. It said, in part:

> Three weeks ago, we lived in Jerusalem in peace and security. Today, Jerusalem is an occupied city ruled by an enemy determined to change its physical appearance and destroy the spirit of its people. Approximately 250 families were bulldozed down in the Moroccan quarter of the Old City. Nearly 3,000 people were made homeless. The immediate danger of starvation faced 30,000 people who lived within the Old City. The deliberate bombing of hospitals in Bethlehem and Jerusalem, the destruction of ambulances by napalm bombs used on retreating soldiers and civilians, were calculated to drive the people from their homes. I appeal to every person to answer this campaign of hatred with a campaign of concern for the Arabs.

For all such voices of conviction and courage, however, through the summer of 1967 and after, ignorance coupled with overwhelming Zionist propaganda warped the reasoning of many intelligent people in the Western world. This was painful to witness, but it also prompted self-criticism among us. A great deal of the fault, we realized, lay with us.

All these years we had failed to speak to the minds of the West with the same aggressiveness that the Zionists brought to the question. We certainly had failed to realize that the West relies on power. Power is more important than justice, violence more effective than reason. Our leaders had been ineffective at wielding either power or reason, and our youth were incensed. In the cities and the camps they recited our failures in ferocious, unsparing verses. We could not protect them from the fiery concepts that inflamed their souls. As Israel started to annex Arab Jerusalem and defy the UN resolutions, contempt for America and Europe was unleashed among our youth.

One week of war had brought destruction to the residential quarters of Jerusalem. During the next week, the Israeli campaign was directed toward the Al-Aqsa Mosque; the inhabitants of the area, about three thousand of them, were forced to evacuate in three days. In the third week, the Israelis completely annexed Jerusalem and dissolved its Arab municipality. World opinion was deaf. Its leaders heard only their own voices.

On August 15, the chief rabbi of Israel climbed up to the Dome of the Rock, one of the most sacred sites of Islam, and conducted a prayer lasting two hours within the confines of the mosque. Then he announced, "This is Jewish property, and we will rebuild the Jewish temple." All of the buildings adjacent to the mosque were demolished. Israeli authorities confiscated the keys to one of the gates of Al-Aqsa. Curfews were forced on people for days. All of these acts humiliated the Islamic world.

Around the same time, a number of freedom fighters had taken refuge in a small verdant camp on the banks of the Jordan River called Karameh. In March 1968, Israeli forces launched a surprise attack on the camp, intending to break the guerrilla forces and clear the area of all resistance. Despite their advanced arms, the Israelis were defeated. The Palestinians pushed back their forces. For the first time, Palestinians felt they could drive the enemy back if they relied on their own power. The battle, which did not last more than fifteen hours, boosted the morale of the Arab fighters. They went back to their orchards and fields fully pledged to fight again. In the refugee camps, the Palestine Liberation Organization (PLO) achieved new stature, and young men in increasing numbers were drawn to its ranks.[3]

Almost a year later, in January 1969, Israeli Gen. Moshe Dayan made a revealing comment to the BBC:

QUESTION: Is there any prospect for peace?
ANSWER: Look here, I did not invent war. There is nothing really new about it. This is apparently the way of war— you fight back until the other party decides that they do not want any more. If you do not fight back, you cannot have peace.

Israel was dizzy with victory. More than that, it was clear that the whole world believed only in military power. The Vietnam War was going full blast. The Vietnamese liberation forces were fighting against the most modern military equipment. They endured suffering, hunger, and disaster in the fight for their country. "Why can't we do the same?" asked our young people. Our youth were angry at everybody and everything. Our softness was weakness to them. We were a failing generation. Had we not failed by trusting the West? By squandering our unity?

In December 1968, Israel launched an unprovoked surprise attack on Beirut Airport, burning thirteen civilian planes to ashes. Of all the Arab countries, Lebanon had been the least involved in the war. The attack on the airport was alarming, but the world appeared to appreciate our efficient and rapid return to normal air service more than the affront to our sovereignty and to international law. With international support, Middle East Airlines resumed its activities immediately. Meanwhile, once again the United Nations condemned Israel, once again Israel turned a deaf ear, and once again the world did nothing.

No wonder an international youth culture spun on its own axis, communicating its impatience and rage, singing its own songs. To me the words of those songs were always superior to the tunes. No melody, however elaborate, could compare with the immortal classical music, which the cultured world continues to cherish and admire. But the new music, whether European or American, told a human story and had an impact on our youngsters. The youth of the world share a common bond. Modern youth music is fascinating in its simplicity. Spontaneous, refreshing, and vibrant, it sings of a new world where human brotherhood is a living expression; it sings of the exuberance of youth in all its moods and often suggests a feeling of triumph over the calamities of life. It is rebellious and boisterous, sometimes bitter, but it is always genuine. Among Palestinians, the youth songs were distinct from those in the West in that they had a strong tone of revenge. Hatred took root among those who had lost everything, and justice became an empty yearning. The martial tunes of revolution eclipsed the old gentle national songs.

"Who taught you to be tough?" goes an Arabic proverb. "My neighbor who died in suffering" is the answer.

XXVI

❧

"SUPPOSE WE BRITISHERS had to accept not only one million but twenty million foreign immigrants, and let us
imagine that these immigrants came to set up their own state
and take over our capital city and the most developed parts of
our country. How would we react? Would we say we can reset-
tle in Canada or Australia? We would all say no matter how
long it will take, no matter what the sacrifices are, London,
Kent and Sussex are British and will be British again. That is
what every people in the world would say."

That was Christopher Mayhew, a British MP, in an appeal for
a just settlement after the 1967 war. His remarks were published
in the newsletter of Americans for Justice in the Middle East
(AJME), which was organized with the intent of enlightening
people in the United States and Europe on the Palestinian situation. Like many who appeared in its pages—prominent writers,
thinkers, and political figures from all over the world—Mayhew
went on to advocate Israeli withdrawal from the occupied territories, enforcement of all UN resolutions on Palestine (a number
of which were newly passed, and ignored, after 1967), and the
right of return or compensation for Palestinians dispossessed

since 1948. It was the responsibility of the world powers, he argued, to induce Israel to withdraw and achieve a settlement. Others, like Anthony Nutting, who had resigned his post as British deputy foreign secretary in 1956 over Suez, argued differently. "According to history, the meek have not inherited the earth," he said, "and the Arabs will never win back Palestine by leaving it to someone else to do the job for them."

The idea animating AJME was that people in the West didn't know the truth about Palestine; if they did, if they heard from noble individuals with the courage to speak out loud for justice, a change would come. A few years earlier, in 1963, the Institute for Palestine Studies had begun with a similar, though far more scholarly, mission: correcting the historical record, lifting the veil that obscured the Palestinian cause, and advancing a scientific approach to all aspects of the problem. For me in this period, working with the Friends of Jerusalem, following the articles produced by AJME and the Institute, strengthened my confidence in people of goodwill.

Others found different means of communicating. After the defeat, university students all over the Arab world rioted. Some sought their share in armed resistance. In the early 1970s, student strikes erupted throughout the occupied territories. Arab relations with Western Europe and America had become extremely strained, and Soviet influence grew in our world. Now the West was calling Israel a bulwark against Communism. Meanwhile, the rich oil states were giving financial backing to the Palestinian commandos. A series of airplane hijackings by commandos put the Palestinian problem on the world's front pages.

Might was making itself felt in all walks of life. Just before he died, in 1970, the great philosopher Bertrand Russell had said, "No people anywhere in the world will accept to be expelled en masse from their own country." Then he asked, "How can anyone expect the people of Palestine to accept a punishment which nobody else would tolerate?" Indeed, the Arabs were sick of tolerance. If we really want to regain our territories, people were saying, then we must fight, "for the world never backs a loser."

All through 1972, President Anwar Sadat tried to appease the restless Egyptian public by promising to retake the occupied territories before the end of the year. His repeated promises only aroused more discontent. Not only in Egypt but in the African Arab states anger was boiling. Sadat's prestige was dwindling. The return of Palestine seemed a far-off dream. Although everyone spoke of fighting, no one felt capable of battling the Israelis.[1] Their army appeared invincible, and their leadership hurled abuse on the Arabs in a provocative manner that none could bear.

Following commando raids from Lebanon into northern Israel, Gen. Moshe Dayan threatened to make southern Lebanon unlivable. The region was bombarded. Villages were demolished, and children, at home while their parents worked in the fields, died under the debris of their shattered dwellings. Every day, it seemed, Israeli soldiers crossed the wire and took hostages into Israel. In a pattern that would repeat all through the 1970s, the Israelis also kidnapped important West Bank citizens and threw them, blindfolded, across the Lebanese frontier. Many Lebanese fishermen disappeared as they chanced to cross Lebanese territorial waters, a designation Israel refused to honor.

Lebanon had no effective army presence in the south, and no one came to the rescue of people whose only fault was living on the border. Tensions between Palestinian refugees and longtime villagers grew. Many villages were deserted, and farmers abandoned their land in a flight for safety. Still others resisted. The more bombing they got, the more resistance they showed and the more sympathy they gained from the Arabs.

So it was a time of humiliation, and our world was both besotted with the warrior and sunk in despair. Through this whole period of the 1960s and 1970s, however, there was another, totally distinct, current of communication. Young people were on the move all over the globe. They were not migrants or refugees but adventurers in search of experience and friends. They came through Lebanon from Europe, America, Africa, and parts of Asia. On the whole they were miserable-looking, underfed, badly dressed, full of perplexities and contradictions, but their sincerity overshadowed their appearance. And they had a glow in their eyes that elicited respect and affection.

With little money, they hitchhiked, walked, cycled, rode trains, or drove fourth-hand cars. I cannot recall the names of most of the young people who stopped in Beirut as they roamed the world, only their countries and their concerns: nonviolence, brotherhood. They came from France, naturally, from Switzerland, Greece, Italy, and Spain; two young men came from Algiers, two women from Bulgaria, three from Serbia, a number from Burma, Singapore, India, and China. The young Japanese spoke of Hiroshima and its profound effect on them.

Two youthful Germans were utterly disgusted with war. They claimed that they had worked in Hitler's headquarters: one as a cook, the other as a guard of honor. The cook, Horst, was the more interesting to our children. Like millions of youth all over Europe during World War II, he was left with no family after his parents died in a raid. But when he spoke, he avoided the personal tragedies and emphasized with moving depth the reality of war. Another visitor I remember well was an American named Pete. He was about twenty-one when we met him in the early 1960s, well built, beaming with vitality and vigor. He had spent a year with Albert Schweitzer and had a great deal to tell our children about the medical missionary. He also offered interesting portraits of Russia and other European countries he had visited, as well as of his home life in the States. In the late 1960s he was engaged in voluntary work in Vietnam, and when he stopped in Beirut, we discussed the horrors of the Asiatic war and the consequences of our own great disaster. Although there was a mass movement against the Vietnam War in the United States, Pete was convinced that average Americans knew as little about the daily reality of Vietnam as they knew about life in Palestine. I recall last hearing from him at Christmas in 1973, from Saigon. That year, the Middle East had again been buffeted by war.

This is how I remember that war. On the morning of October 6, 1973, my husband and I left Brummana with the intention of moving back to Beirut for the winter. The countryside was quiet as we took the hill road down to the coast. We saw two planes approaching the airport. When we reached the city, it was calm. Then in the afternoon the radio had news—loud and obscure. The words seemed to come from the other side of the world. We could not follow them for the blur. Outside, balconies filled with people, everyone questioning his neighbor. The news from Egypt and Syria spread like a flame.

We could not believe the reports of a successful crossing of the Suez Canal by Egyptian forces. We doubted that Egyptian and Syrian battalions were advancing into the occupied territories. From 1967 on, the foreign press had glorified the Israeli military as having no weaknesses. Now the picture was starting to change. The television brought scenes of Israeli soldiers being taken prisoner. We looked hard, trying to convince ourselves of the authenticity of the information.

These were headlines in the world news: "Waves of Egyptian commandos crossed the canal in rubber boats, climbed the defenses with ladders and destroyed key Israeli positions." "The Barlev Line has been destroyed by the Egyptians."[2] "Egyptian soldiers built floating bridges and successfully crossed the canal." "Kuneitra, the most important city in the Golan Heights, has been liberated."

The Israelis tried to deny many of these reports, but the pictures in the press seemed as real as the morning sun. We were told at the start that the Syrians were aided by the Palestinians. In the course of the war, the Israelis put greater pressure on Syria than on Egypt. They tried to get to Damascus, and their radio falsely announced that the capital had fallen. During the third week, military operations slowed down, and there was a general feeling that Israel had more big-power backing and superior arms. But the gains the Arabs did make were enough to convince the Arab armies that Israeli invincibility was a myth. If not now, someday in the near future they would reclaim the lost territories.

Egypt's Sadat and Syria's Hafez al-Assad grew tremendously in prestige as a result of this short war. Above all else, the sense of shame disappeared, and our youth had a feeling of rebirth. Like the battle of Karameh but on a larger scale, the 1973 war brought a psychological victory. Everyone had underestimated the will of the Arabs to fight back. In a press conference a few hours before the surprise attack, Moshe Dayan had said, "Calm reigns on the banks of Suez. The lines are secure, the bridges are open. Our political situation is firm. All this is the result of a balanced, daring, and longsighted policy."

Now the question remained: could there be a political settlement? With the joint agreement of Russia and the United States, the Security Council had voted for a cease-fire on October 21. It stipulated that a joint committee for peace be established to implement UN Resolution 242, calling for the withdrawal of Israel from the occupied territories.

President Sadat had given a remarkable speech urging the Americans and Russians to be sensitive to justice and to force Israel to abide by the resolution. His words were carefully chosen, and there was no anger in his tone. He emphasized that the battle of 1973 was fought over Egyptian territories and that the Arabs wanted only to regain their lost lands. Sadat spoke of the suffering and fright among the people, and promised to put an end to all this.

By contrast, Israeli Prime Minister Golda Meir gave a summary of events and insisted that though some damage had been done to the Arab armies, Israel was bent on breaking their backs. Thousands of her men were fighting in a desert land that did not belong to them. Why was she driving them to further agony? As I listened to her sour words, I wondered if she ever experienced the loss of a son in battle.

The 1973 war was virtually over when the Security Council announced its final resolution. The Israelis formally accepted it but refused to accept the cease-fire. From Monday, October 22, to Friday of that week, shooting continued in localized areas in the Canal Zone. On October 27 the United States announced the mobilization of its units all over the world. This came in response to the Russians, who had declared that they were ready to come to the aid of the Arabs. The Soviet Union had proposed a peacekeeping force of Soviet and U.S. units to observe the implementation of Resolution 242—that is, Israeli withdrawal to its pre-1967 borders—but the Americans refused. It appeared that this would not be the last war.

Two positive results came out of 1973. First was the realization that Arab oil could be an effective weapon against the imperial pressure of the United States and Europe. Shortly after the war began, King Faisal of Saudi Arabia and then all the Arab oil states announced they were cutting oil supplies to the United States and certain European countries. As the largest producer of oil in the world, Saudi Arabia was pivotal here. The other notable result was the decision of twenty-nine African states to cut relations with Israel, which discovered that its occupation of Arab lands was not a passport to peace but a gateway to more insecurity and isolation.

Diplomatic activities continued between the superpowers as well as among the Arab countries. The presidents of Algeria, Libya, Egypt, and Syria met again in Saudi Arabia under the leadership of Faisal, who accelerated the oil boycott. The possibility of a second war of attrition loomed. Then on November 16 a vague agreement on a cease-fire was signed. It was not exactly peace. By February of 1974 the complete disengagement of Egyptian and Israeli troops from the Canal Zone was put into effect. But Israel had continued to breach cease-fire lines and had not withdrawn to its pre-1967 borders. As of April 1974, the Syrians were still fighting in the Golan Heights, trying to regain their lost positions on the summits of Mt. Hermon. In Beirut, every once in a while we heard the thundering sound of military planes falling into the sea across the southern border. Egypt was still in a state of unrest, as the canal would not be cleared and reopened to world traffic for another year. This effort to reopen the canal created a great deal of commercial activity in Beirut, as European contractors made their way to the East awaiting opportunities and big enterprise.

The fundamental balance of power, though, was unchanged, as was the plight of the Palestinians. The United States appeared willing to disrupt the whole world and endanger its economy for the sake of Israeli intransigence. In 1974 U.S. Senator J. William Fulbright stated that "Israeli reprisals against the Palestinians have been pitiless and horrible," and he deplored "the indifference of the press to the routine savagery of the Israeli reprisals while they make great issues of Palestinian reprisals." Fulbright cautioned the Americans:

> It is because of us and us alone that Israel has come into being as a state. At least now Israel must realize that we cannot stake more to have her continue to exist through violence at the expense of her neighbors.

Fulbright was a maverick, though, and never represented the consensus of the U.S. government on the issue. President Richard Nixon had raised American arrogance to unbearable heights. U.S. Middle East policy would be eclipsed later that year by the Watergate scandal, but after Nixon resigned, it would not be reoriented to achieve a just and lasting settlement in Palestine. By the close of 1974 it seemed that national survival was the Palestinians' achievement. They would resist. They would not go away. They would not be obliterated. As the Palestinian scholar Edward Said[3] wrote in *Newsweek* that December:

> To the People of Israel:
> Although I was deeply saddened by the Arab defeat in 1967, I was also puzzled by what you would do after your victory. Its ritualism had been a bad first sign: the rams' horns blowing, the proclamations about unfulfilled prophecy, the immobile self-righteousness, the eloquence hiding a vacant, and often astoundingly coarse and brutal, policy. For from 1967 on you disastrously mishandled your victory. Every Arab statement was dismissed either with open scorn or with a barrage of purposely

humiliating demands. You held what seemed to be epicurean debates about us, even as your Egyptian, Lebanese, Jordanian and Syrian raids, sometimes wanton in their violence and brilliant only in their calculated sadistic cruelty, gained you stiffened Arab resistance on the one hand or increasing world isolation on the other. In your official policy of ignoring the Palestinian people, on whose subjugation Israel now stands, you focused our will and clarified our patriotic struggle.

Future events proved the truth of those words.

XXVII

~

A T THE END of the academic year of 1974, I retired from my
job as school principal and started what I believed would
be a new life of ease. My career had been most enriching, and
the school was in good hands. As I left the office where I had
spent forty happy years of my life, every little book, every map
and picture meant a great deal to me. My office was spacious
and quiet. Often I had stayed into the late hours enjoying the
tranquillity of study and thought. The hundred boarders, the
staff, and the whole atmosphere inspired warmth and solidarity.
This place was a corner of heaven to me. Here I had been sub-
merged in ideas, here I had dreamed beautiful dreams, and here
I had tried to achieve. The school was a home, not only to me
but also to the thousands of others who had experienced its
harmonious community. Our anxieties and fears, our sorrows
and joys, our expectations and aspirations, were translated into
blissful action. Life here was an expression of faith, hope, and
love—above all, love.

That summer in Brummana was delightful, filled with the
fragrance of the flowering bushes in our mountain garden. We
had two loving grandchildren and were expecting more. Living

with children, listening to their precious talk, their golden dreams, is an experience of unique value in our troubled world.

And yet, as gratified as I was by my family and my achievements at the Ahliah School, I could not help feeling that we, the older people who claimed to be the guardians of a civilization, had let our young ones down. Nonviolence was our calling, but the world we bequeathed taught them that violence is the more trusted companion of their dreams. That summer the American University had been closed for more than a month after a student body full of political discontent disrupted its academic life. There had been many other strikes across the university's hundred-year history—strikes in favor of teaching the medical sciences in Arabic, strikes in favor of teaching Darwin's theory of evolution or accepting new scientific ideas. This strike became violent as the government called in the police. It was painful to see armed forces keeping guard over university gates through which many thousands of young men and women had walked into the wide world armed with knowledge and truth. A number of wise professors tried to smooth relations between the students and the administration. Sadly, the clash deepened as the security forces entered the university gates.

The university had been changed by the tragedy of 1967. We who had known it as a haven of spiritual strength were deeply disturbed to see it turn into an instrument of political ambition. This university had been founded by men who lived above the conflicts of their times. Money and power had never counted for much with them; service to mankind was their noblest goal. How far we stand from them now! True, our ancestors did not see the Arab countries torn to bits to please the colonial powers. And in their age the creation of a Zionist state was a far-fetched notion.

Now our youth, our country, seemed to be going to the rocks. The Palestinians living within our borders felt repudiated by the whole world, strangers even among their own people. Our government in Lebanon was callous, corrupt, and indifferent. Only a few hands wielded power, and among the people there was a great restlessness.[1]

Gangs of outlaws beset the northern town of Tripoli, and the army used a great deal of force to suppress crime. In the south, Israeli forces continued to destroy villages and drive civilians from their homes, while government leaders answered them with talk and more talk. Our newspapers mentioned little about the cruelties suffered by the south; in many instances these were completely ignored. The television busily distracted the people with "Tric Trac," or backgammon, competitions. Our president would meet Syria's president at the borders, and broadcasts from both countries were warm and reassuring. King Faisal shuttled from country to country in the region, and so did Henry Kissinger, back and forth, feeding us small doses of hope. But beneath the surface one could sense the embers of a hidden fire.

The winter of 1975 was exceptionally severe. The mountain areas suffered a terrible snowstorm, resulting in many casualties and great material loss. Torrential rains on the coast caused destructive flooding. It seemed like a punishment to those of us who were indifferent to the trials endured by the south. March continued to be stormy, with unprecedented fierce rains. But April was sunny and radiant, and that is when the civil war began.

On April 13 fighting erupted in the suburbs of Beirut between Palestinians and right-wing Phalangist Christians. In no time the whole city was engulfed. From its start, our civil war was savage. The hearts of the warriors of both camps, so-called Muslim and Christian militias, were bursting with black anger. The majority of the population, feeling powerless, retreated into the background. The country became prey to insane youth whose true desire was to play havoc with everything.

A lull in the fighting at the beginning of summer brought a wave of optimism that the war was over. Our daughter, Mariam, and her family came from the States to visit in June; by August, when they left, the country was again tense. Within hours of their departure, Beirut was on fire. We were in Brummana, amid its refreshing breezes, but every day we followed the death toll in the papers. It all sounded unreal. The official radio took up responsibility for helping people get from place to place in Beirut. The announcers gave the names of the roads and the level of safety along the way to the gates of the city. It was a sincere enough idea, but it simply fed the feeling of perpetual danger. No one left home except in extreme necessity. Many unarmed people were shot. East and West Beirut became hardened enclaves, with Christians in the east, Muslims and Palestinian refugees in the west, and intense combat across what eventually was called the Green Line.

The early battles seemed aimed at dividing the capital and destroying it. Everywhere snipers caused horror. Parts of Beirut became deserted. Those who had means traveled far, to Europe or the States. Others went to Syria or Iraq, but most people had no choice but to stay and suffer. As the months passed, the country was paralyzed with unproductivity and unemployment, as fewer people dared to go to work. The fighting spread like a devouring fire. Hardly a corner was spared. From the business areas, the fighting moved into the hotels and spread into the heart of Beirut.

I worried greatly about my husband, Emile, who had to cross the line, though his factory was far from the hottest zone. My son Sami's office was near the Kantari region, a center of Beirut that was wild with danger. The American University hospital, where my eldest son, Nadim, worked, was safer. Nadim was part of a small team of doctors who continued to work under the most adverse conditions, treating hundreds of wounded and maimed patients. As he walked to the hospital every morning, we worried about him and impatiently awaited his return. He always went again in the afternoons. Of all of us, he came into closest contact with the young fighters. Night and day, he lived with their fears and rage. We heard so many awful stories that I'm afraid we even became a bit insensitive to life and death. Fortunately these overburdened doctors labored to rescue what could be rescued.

As Christmas approached, it was evident the war was beyond control. Fighting raged in the north and south. All roads to the capital were blocked. Telephones were dead. In Beirut we lived for days with no water or with contaminated water, and no electricity whatsoever. We used great quantities of candles. Food was available, except for bread. A number of bakeries could not function because they had been damaged by bombs. Hundreds of women and children died in the crowded sections near the bakeries.

The only thing that operated with a certain regularity was the press. Our daily papers continued to circulate, their reports spreading more panic among the people. As there was effectively no government, the press enjoyed maximum freedom. All shades of doctrine reached us, adding to our confusion. Indeed, in some reports the battles sounded more frightful than anything we had heard from Vietnam or any other war zone. What a horrid feeling of insecurity! It seemed that anybody could die at any minute, no matter where he happened to be. Blind bullets fell upon us like rain.

I felt especially disturbed when a radio announcer spoke of "strangers" waging war against the Lebanese. He was referring to the Palestinians. Had we forgotten that this was a civil war? We, who had always considered Lebanon an integral part of the Arab world, a place where human horizons could expand freely—we were talking about "strangers"?

Beirut had been the warmest city on the Mediterranean coast. People from every clime had made it their home and taken pride in it. Despite its anarchy, it once was the center of a relaxed and happy society. Here, journalists, writers, and holiday-makers, tourists from all over the world, speaking different languages and belonging to various nationalities, had found a haven of liberal thinking and living. For the longest time everybody had found friendship and affection. As Pasternak wrote, "In the Kingdom of God there are no citizens." I had always believed this. We were not a people who had thought in terms of national barriers. How could we have "strangers" among us trampling our future when "strangers" were once the heart of our community?

XXVIII

~

A Wartime Diary

SEPTEMBER 1975

There are more birds on our veranda today. Every day there are more. They pick up the grains we put out for them, their daily bread. Everybody is busy with the war. People are killing each other in a pointless struggle that gets us nowhere. I wonder when the birds will warble again in the few trees of our neighborhood. Now they take their meals and disappear. Like us, they are frightened of the men who fight one another.

NOVEMBER 1975

Alarming news. Our daughter-in-law Asdghik was shot in the legs by a sniper on one of the main crossings of the city. She was driving with Nadim to visit a patient in a hospital in the eastern section. Thanks to immediate medical care, her life was spared. Thank God it all ended well. She is expecting her first baby.

JANUARY 1976

The New Year started badly for many people, especially those who had hidden their jewelry in safe deposit boxes. The banks have been robbed. Looting has occurred everywhere. We have been told that professional looters come from distant places to pillage the treasures of Beirut. Who knows? Beirut was once a rich city.

Fighting has started raging in the hinterland. The sale of arms is expanding on both sides, and so are corruption in arms dealing and illegal wealth. Money is a mighty god. Our pseudo-Parliament is crippled as corruption spreads into wider spheres of society. There are daily shameful stories of men in power making money over the bodies of innocent victims. No one seems to care that the country is going to pieces. New militias of every kind and temperament have sprouted up to sow panic in an already divided army and country. If you ask the young fighters what they are fighting for, they have no clear answer. This applies to all. We civilians have nothing to rely upon. Our faith in our weak army wavers day by day.

Many people have become fatalistic. Merchants whose stores were demolished bring their goods into the residential areas and handle business for a few hours as peddlers. In the morning the streets are full of commodities, but by noon the city is lifeless. Not a soul is outdoors in the afternoon, not even in the streets where enormous numbers once pursued a livelihood.

With big wooden crosses on their breasts, the so-called Christian militias are fighting savagely. Their intention is to empty poor areas of their inhabitants. On the eighteenth they attacked the Karantina district without mercy. Men were massacred, while the women and children were taken as hostages to unknown areas. We're hearing a thousand may be dead. Mass slaughter has been the story since "Black Saturday" [December 6, 1975], when the Phalangists shot into Muslim crowds, killing hundreds in a few hours. They set up roadblocks, demanding to see identity cards. Palestinians, stateless and without these cards, were killed in cold blood, as were Muslims.

Accounts of the PLO's retaliatory attacks on the Christian towns of Damour and Gie are equally horrible. Damour was a model town, a garden city with lovely quaint houses and orchards, where oranges, mandarins, lemons, and bananas grew in large quantities. The displaced people of Karantina made their way toward Damour, and thus the line of danger stretched farther along the coast to the south. Hundreds were killed in Damour; a great deal of greenery has been burned to ash, and the luscious orchards have been ravished. Now the cleavage between the different religious factions has become deeper, as people are leaving their homes to find safety or doom among their own "kind."

SPRINGTIME 1976

Nature is blooming in the city as well as in the mountains. The almond and apricot trees are glossy on the heights. The pines give a velvety verdure to the hills around. All seems breathtakingly beautiful in our lovely country, but man is ugly and evil. The days are marked with constant bombing; the nights are eerie. We never would have imagined we could live through this. My cousin Mona arrived from Brummana, and her presence is a real delight. Like a blooming flower of April, she brings an aroma of sweetness to every member of the family. Even the plants are refreshed by her arrival. Her clever hands make pretty things, and all the children love her dearly. With an ever-generous heart, she has taken us all under her loving care.

APRIL 21, 1976

In this painful atmosphere a bit of happiness! Our daughter-in-law has given birth to a lovely baby boy. Little Samer has flooded our world with jubilation. All of a sudden the days no longer seem meaningless; they sparkle. Thus wrote Tagore for every child on earth, in his "Crescent Moon":

He has come to this land of a hundred crossroads
Clasp him to your heart and bless him.
He will follow you laughing and not a doubt in his heart.
Though the waves underneath grow threatening
Yet the breath from above may waft him to the haven of peace.
Forget him not in your hurry, let him come to your heart and
  bless him.

MAY 1976

Beirut is being bombarded daily. We are grateful that the baby sleeps peacefully through the diabolic sound of the rockets. Several nights we have slept in the corridors to avoid the noise. It rattles our nerves. But when we wake up in the morning, a new world is revealed in the baby's smiling face.

MAY 22, 1976

We gave a birthday party for Emile. He is 74. The whole family and friends—we were about fifty people—joined in wishing him all the best. It was a relaxing, cheerful occasion. Emile has been a solid rock in this stormy sea. He seems to carry the burdens of everyone on his broad shoulders and sustains us all with his overflowing optimism. I am not sure who is more optimistic, Emile or Cousin Fadlo, who works with him in the factory, but they complement each other admirably. I wait for Fadlo's morning visits just to be cheered up. He has a blend of humor and spiritual wisdom in his conversation, and also faith in my husband's life work, that I so appreciate. His presence has given Emile the peace of mind and strength to continue making future plans for the factory. While everything around has gone to ruin, factory production has continued, thanks to the few faithful workers whose sense of duty is stronger than the hurricanes of violence. I cannot conceive of life without Emile's fortitude, courage, and care. May God give him strength for many years to come.

JUNE 1976

We are standing at the doors of hell. We hear stories of abduction and revenge. How long will this continue? No one knows. Some schools tried to reopen, but almost no one has the peace of mind to undertake regular work. The battles of the refugee camps seem endless and have a ferocity that surpasses imagination. In the mountains, in the villages, at the crossing points between East and West Beirut, everything gets hotter. Broadcasts on the unofficial radio bands are vindictive and mean. There are constant appeals from the official radio for peace, but no one listens to the voice of authority. Authority has abdicated its role.

JUNE 8, 1976

We celebrated the birthday of my sister Selma with a small group of the family. Selma is much like Emile in these turbulent days: brave. She has a fantastic memory and cheers us up with stories from the past that are full of humor. With old age, Selma has acquired new dimensions of wisdom. I have always valued her sound judgment and deep understanding of life but never so much as now. Simple in her habits, simple in her wants, she is an emblem of serenity in a world of greed.

My sister Soumaya has taken her seven grandchildren to Baghdad. It was strenuous at her advanced age of seventy-five to carry the little ones all the way from their parents in Beirut, but, like Selma, she has always been willing to forget herself when it comes to others. And she is determined. The children, she felt, must get out.

SUMMER 1976

The beautiful Koura region, where my grandparents had lived, is in turmoil. It has been severely hit by militias from the north. Some 26,000 citizens have left their homes and taken refuge in Tripoli. In Beirut our balconies are full of shrapnel. With death knocking at many doors in our neighborhood, I have been thinking of Tagore's last poem, "On Wings of Death." I have always loved Tagore:

> Every morning in the gracious touch of light
> I receive the homage of existence
> My bloodstream merges in the stream of light.
> Sweet is the world and sweet the dust of it
> Death cannot swallow Life which is immortal.
> Death has lost all its terrors for me, it is new birth
> May the bonds of Earth dissolve,
> The mighty Universe take me to her arms
> And I come to know fearlessly
> The Great Unknown.

JUNE 24, 1976

The airport has reopened. It was closed for seventeen days, and we felt cut off from all the world then. The airport had been shelled more than once. One shelling caused the death of a pilot. None of the passengers was hit, but the brave, unlucky pilot met his death while saving the plane. In revenge, on Sunday night, the left and the Palestinians shelled Jouniyeh from

Beirut, and people in that isolated harbor were terrified by many casualties.

JUNE 27, 1976

The airport is closed again after having been heavily bombarded. When the airport was attacked, about 800 people were in the area planning to travel. Now again we are completely isolated from the world.

JUNE 30, 1976

The battle of the camps continues for the ninth day. It is ferocious beyond words. Our leaders are resting in their relatively secure dwellings, scheming more evil for the hundreds of youngsters who are utterly exposed to destruction. Men of old used to fight with pistols. They did not kill the innocent civilians who were far from the fighting areas. How uncivilized we are compared with our ancestors.

There is an attempt to use the sea route to get fuel oil to Beirut. Things are still dreadfully confused. We are in a state of siege; bread is not available. Some housewives waited for six hours in a queue and got five loaves of bread. Then gunmen broke the queues and took their share. People have been telling a story about an old woman who had been waiting for some time; when she discovered how effective the gun was at getting bread, she pleaded with the gunmen to let her borrow it.

JULY 15, 1976

A frightful battle has been fought in and around the gardens of the camp areas. At one time countless cars came there to pick up heaps of flower bunches to sell in the city market. Who wants to buy flowers when a bloody war is raging in the neighborhood?

Who wants to look at flowers when men kill one another with abandon? We are turning into beasts.

Social life continues because otherwise we would go mad. The Zurayks come often to see us. Costi's deep sense of justice, his sound intellectual thinking, his meticulous sense of honesty, do not help cheer us up, though. His vision of the future is gray and often dark. Najla is full of warmth, and their girls radiate optimism. Their breathless youth is our anchor; there is something visionary in it. My cousin Nida also entertains us with her merry laughter. She frets about the war but avoids speaking of it. She recounts humorous incidents from her life instead and chatters about her houseplants and flowers, her colorful paintings, her remodeled furniture, and her delight in all things bright and beautiful. She comes as sunny relief.

AUGUST 1976

At the start of August there was a brief feeling of ease as we heard of an attempted peace agreement. It supposedly involved disarmament and a stipulation that the wounded and captives in the camps would be taken care of. There is no evidence that such an agreement has been respected. On the twelfth, Palestinians in the Tal al-Zaatar camp in East Beirut were subject to wholesale slaughter. For two months they had been under siege by Christian militias and government forces backed by Syria; now we are hearing this was a massacre, thousands killed, refugees cut down by machine guns.

There is talk of changing our boundaries. Changing boundaries is one of the desired objectives of all wars everywhere. After this terrible civil war of ours, we may be forced to acquiesce to such changes. Was the loss of thousands upon thousands of young men worth this? Have we not progressed to any stage of reasonable thinking? Why can't we change boundaries without bloodshed?

The Mediterranean is placid on this bright summer morning. The sky is clear, with patches of white clouds. Beautiful trees encircle many parts of the city. At one time this place was alluring, the envy of the world.

SEPTEMBER 23, 1976

The night was calm with sporadic shooting. The president-elect, Ilyas Sarkis, is supposed to be sworn in by Parliament in Chtaura, Bekaa, today. Bekaa is a Syrian-held territory, and many deputies are making excuses not to attend.[1] We all hope that Sarkis will take a strong stand. We are worried for him because he has not shown any knowledge of intrigue. He seems honest and straightforward. The ex-president was corrupt. We all wonder whether Sarkis can overcome a crippled Parliament and a hated predecessor. The meeting is to take place at noon. Hope is our only escape from fear.

LATER, SEPTEMBER 23

President-elect Sarkis gave a balanced speech. We have reason to be optimistic. He spoke frankly and sincerely of his desire to see Lebanon on its feet again. He appealed to the youth of the country and emphasized that much is asked of them to form a new state, a state not based on religious denominations and sects but on merit and hard work. He spoke with dignity about the Palestinians and their cause. He emphasized the Arab character of Lebanon. The Palestinian command has declared a cease-fire.

SEPTEMBER 28, 1976

We have been constantly startled by armed men who want to confiscate our apartment building. Nadim and Selma are making contacts to keep the place intact. The two doctors in the building are away in the States. The atmosphere is tense. A few bombs rocked Ras-Beirut yesterday, in the morning and at night. The mountain battle in which the Syrian forces are engaged continues. The election of Sarkis did not change the situation much. We are still hopeful, although our nerves are at their end.

OCTOBER 1976

There is some optimism in the air. Apparently there was an Arab summit in Riyadh, Saudi Arabia, including Egypt, Syria, Kuwait, and the Palestinian resistance. Lebanon was not asked to attend. This war has weakened Lebanon's position beyond imagination. It may take us years before we recover. Let us hope the military part is over. Syria is going to interfere more and more with our destiny, but in the present situation we have little choice. Even an unambitious peace is better than a state of blood and fright.

OCTOBER 20, 1976

Fighting continues. Rockets rain on Beirut's residential areas. Around 6 p.m., three strong rockets fell in our neighborhood and did a great deal of material damage. We are extremely lucky not to have been hit. We seem to be a target and feel panicky.

The warring factions are still fighting in the mountain area. Autumn is so beautiful there. The colorful leaves have not fallen as yet. Some trees are still laden with the gifts of the season, but no one is able to go to his farm and pick his fruits or vegetables. Man is afraid of his brother man.

Today Beirut reminds me of ancient Rome, which was often described as a turbulent city. Diverse gatherings of people of all races and creeds, people who cherish various values and speak different languages are all here. Each section governs itself as best it can. But as a society Beirut has lost its pride and self-respect, and no one seems to care. Poverty and misery are hiding while audacious money-mongers are amassing wealth. How degrading.

JANUARY 1977

The military war is over, but the New Year brings apprehension. The city is partitioned, Muslim/Christian; the country divided. At the heart of Beirut the old city is ruined beyond recognition. Its fashionable hotels and the mighty structures and skyscrapers sweeping its boulevards fell to the ground, and it does not seem they will be able to rise up again. A number of them have crumbled to dust. Where do we begin? Many cities have been devastated like this by earthquakes, but Beirut has suffered a deep injury inflicted by our own hands. The damage we have done to our capital is almost inconceivable.

None of our family experienced a major material loss or sudden calamity during the war. Death came as a loving angel to carry away two of our elderly members. One dear old lady passed away peacefully during the fighting but could not be cremated or buried, as fuel was out of reach and the cemetery was in a danger zone outside the city limits. At the end of the war, Uncle Anis, who was over ninety, passed away and had a grand funeral in the chapel of the university, where he spent fifty years of his fruitful life. Other families were not as lucky as ours. Everywhere, people in black cross the streets wearing looks of despair, not knowing where or how their sons died. This is agony in its most heartbreaking form.

Many children were confined indoors during the war. They must feel jubilant to be set free again. Even in winter they will remember the sun. Some children have not seen the sun for many months. They will remember the trees and flowers and the sea. During the battles, they would peep through small windows to watch the movements of rebellious troops. They learned the names of all kinds of arms. They forgot that there are more interesting things in life than death.

OCTOBER 1977

I'm afraid hatred has not vanished from the hearts of men. Perhaps it is sharper than ever. Hatred breeds hatred, just as love breeds love. The children lived a long time with horrible stories, and I think it will take more than one generation to obliterate the effects of this ravaging war. If our children cannot live in a world better than our own, perhaps their children can. That prospect alone keeps our hope alive.

DECEMBER 1977

It feels like history is turning backward everywhere now that I read about Bokassa crowning himself emperor of the Central African Empire. It used to be called a republic. With opulence beyond measure in a country where poverty, want, and ignorance are features of everyday life, Bokassa imitated Napoleon I in a festival that broke the back of his people. Twentieth-century Africans suffer to satisfy the false pride of a lunatic. The so-called civilized world is silent about it.

Can we not express world resentment? The country's former French colonial masters sent a battalion to guard the ceremony. Bokassa may be insane, but his uranium is useful. How cowardly we all are.

XXIX

~

M Y FATHER OFTEN SAID, "There was a great deal of good in 'the old world,' but we were too blind to see it. We were lured by the magic machine, spellbound by power, and forgot the spirit behind the machine." I was a child of five when World War I started. Before that, from what my parents told me, people felt that we were living in an orderly world, moving progressively into a better future. Poverty and illness were receding. Medicine was alleviating suffering; life seemed safer, easier, and more wondrous thanks to science. At least it had that prospect.

The war of 1914 upset the peaceful life. It is not that the world had no ugliness, hatred, and jealousy before, but with the war those grew deeper in the hearts of mankind, rivalries expanded, and material gain became the most important measure of life. Public respect went to the rich and aggressive. The world did not become "safer for democracy," as the slogan had it. And it was not "the war to end all wars." In the world of my birth, the world I loved, it was the beginning of endless war. War has crowded the memories of my youth and old age and every stage in between.

I lived through our terrible civil war when I was in my late sixties. I thought, Surely this has to be the end of it. And in November of 1977 there was something exciting in the news, a breakthrough: the decision of Egypt's President Sadat to negotiate openly for peace with Israel. Sadat's courageous trip to Jerusalem monopolized the news. If he succeeded, the Arabs would score a victory. The Arab world was divided as to the wisdom of the trip, but public opinion at large responded positively to the move. Israel had not taken seriously countless UN resolutions, and we in contrast had stacked all of our hopes on those resolutions. Here was something new.

A few months later, on March 15, 1978, the old returned with a vengeance. An Israeli army detachment estimated at about 30,000 men invaded southern Lebanon. This left us speechless! For more than ten years the south had been the target of Israeli attacks, its hardworking peasants subjected to intimidation and kidnapping. This time the invasion was on a larger scale. As part of the Lebanese peace accord, the Palestinian fighters had left Beirut and settled in the south. It was as if no one would be satisfied unless they were exterminated. Several peaceful villages were completely destroyed, and a quarter-million refugees swarmed into the cities. Sidon and Beirut were inundated by homeless families. Tyre was under constant bombing. Miserable women, children, and elders drifted aimlessly to nowhere.

A week before the invasion, a Palestinian commando squad crossed the wire into Israel and hijacked two buses. Thirty-seven Israeli civilians were killed in the Palestinian assault; in response, Israel used its most brutal conventional weaponry to destroy a vast swath of Lebanon's territory. The only resistance to the invasion came from the Palestinian guerrillas. They fought back bravely, controlling the advance of the Israeli army and preventing it from taking the coastal city of Tyre. There was a slight tone of reprimand in the U.S. response to the Israeli invasion, but the strongest objection came from the United Nations. It demanded the immediate withdrawal of Israeli troops and stationed an international police force on the border.

From March 22 through the first week of April, Beirut became the refuge of nearly 300 homeless families. Some returned to the south soon after that, but the Israelis occupy their lands and refuse to withdraw to their former frontiers.

So here we are. For more than sixty years the world has been going mad. Not the honest nor the brave but the mighty have been its masters. For as long as I have lived, powerful men have authored death and extermination or the means to threaten it, and have perverted science for this aim. They carved up the Middle East to satisfy their whims and their greed, and then watched as the forces they set in motion worked toward a seemingly inevitable disintegration. Colonialism taught its lessons too well. For all their power and wealth the imperial nations of Europe were not able to avoid two world wars; the nations they created by drawing lines on a map or issuing declarations have done the same but more modestly, with regional wars, civil wars, occupations. The Arab world is insecure. Despite its nuclear weapons, Israel is insecure. No border is ever secure without mutual trust and understanding.

Our governments are the deformed products of their hard birth. When some of the Arab countries asked for independence, cruel conditions were exacted from them. We in Lebanon were promised freedom in 1943. When our pseudo government expressed a slight tendency for a reasonable portion of it, our French colonizers stationed Senegalese soldiers in our streets to plant fear. Our first government was immediately exiled and replaced by a pro-French cabinet. Foreign troops remained on our land until the start of 1946. By then, Europe was too weak to dictate orders to us, but throughout the colonized world freedom had to be purchased with blood, and everywhere, as if it were the first rule of statecraft, people had been left with examples of power through theft.

All over the world, a rebellious element came to the fore. It tried to right past wrongs, but as time has moved on, it has become embittered and mean. The strong exhibit selfishness in its most repulsive shades. They ridicule order. The roots of a disciplined society desiccate, and our promising world withers. The civil war in Lebanon gave me a horrible feeling of despair. The young keep nourishing their faith with fresh hopes, but not the old. Those ugly battles stole away my dreams. Peace is the essence of all my aspirations now. This troubled area of ours is tired of war. It has ruined the loveliest expressions of our lives.

Will the strong nations allow us to bandage our bleeding wounds? Will Israel be allowed to continue to do whatever it wants? Will our youth free themselves from fanaticism and rebuild the land of our fathers with the sweat of honest labor? Will they ever see justice? These questions torture my soul. The beauty of Lebanon is not enough to make us forget the folly of this war we have just endured. Our purple mountains against the clear skies, their white peaks reflecting light on the verdant hills, the flowers of the fields, the limpid streams, will continue to feed our souls. Spring will come again with its perfume and color and remind us of nature's immeasurable gifts. Do we deserve all this? Our generation has failed to bring men nearer to one another. Will the new generation prove wiser?

Afterword

୬

NAJLA SAID

Like anyone who loses a grandmother at the age of five, I remember Teta Wadad in vague, visceral ways. I remember the tea she drank in the afternoon with milk and sugar. I remember the way she sat, like a lady, with her legs together and placed neatly to her side, sometimes crossed at the ankle. I remember the tight, tidy bun in which she wrapped her long hair every day, the lap she let me sit in, and the stories she would read to me. One of my clearest memories of my early childhood is of Teta tucking me into bed on the first night of one of our summers in Beirut. I must have been three or four. My parents, my older brother, Wadie, and I had arrived after our long flight from New York, exhausted and weary. My uncle Sami carried me into the house on his shoulders, and after I was given a bath, Wadie and I settled in for the night. Teta perched herself at the edge of my bed, and Wadie and I nestled in next to her. She opened a big book and began to read to us. I remember that there were lots of elaborate colored pictures in the book and that the pages seemed massive next to my (and

Teta's) tiny hands. While I don't remember much of the story, except that God featured prominently in it, I do recall staring, awed and transfixed by the illustration of Him as she read. The depiction of God was a very warm and kind-looking old man, with gray hair and long, lovely robes. He sat on a throne and held a golden staff. All of the world's living creatures were gathered around Him—horses, giraffes, birds, dogs, fish, human beings—and by the way Teta read to us I knew that He was a loving and benevolent old man who would always take care of me. Thirty years later, years filled with education and spiritual exploration, I find that this image of God has stayed with me, etched indelibly in my mind. When my father passed away, I imagined him safe with the old man in the chair. When I have needed to turn to someone for guidance, I imagined the old man in the chair listening patiently to, and answering, all of my questions. Although I am fully aware that this rather quaint, childlike image of the Lord is not very politically correct in this day and age, I cling to it. And I remember Teta's warm, expressive voice reading to me.

What occurs to me, in trying to write about Teta, is how few of us have the opportunity to really know our grandparents as people. Grandparents, to little children, often seem to serve no purpose other than to be givers of unconditional, pure love (and, often, presents). As a child, Teta Wadad was, to me, just my teta. After she died in 1979, memories of her and of war-ravaged Lebanon faded in my mind. Teta became part of a warm memory, her image a comforting reminder of a lost world.

Teta wrote this memoir during her last years, as civil war raged around her, forever changing the landscape of the country she had known and loved her whole life. She ends the book not only distraught at the ravages of war but also deeply concerned by the "hatred in the hearts of men." Teta's fear is for the future generations: Will they succeed in finding peace, or fail, as she feels her generation has done?

After her death, we continued yearly visits to Lebanon as a family, staying away only when the situation was really dire, such as the summer of 1982. In an unsuccessful bid to decimate the PLO, the Israelis invaded Lebanon that summer. We returned a year later, when I was nine years old, only to be forced to evacuate on a boat to Cyprus as bombs fell into the sea around us. I did not return to Lebanon again until 1992, two years after the civil war ended. I hated every minute of it. The warm and loving world I remembered was gone, everything was dust and rubble, anger and tension were prevalent, and most of my loved ones had grown old or died. I remember feeling that it didn't seem at all fair to have lost a home; that it was unjust that it wasn't safe for my father, a Palestinian, to even be there. I, like Teta in the last pages of her book, began to doubt even if God existed; if so, he was not the benevolent old man I envisioned.

But then, after systematically destroying every last piece of their country, the Lebanese rebuilt. Just like that. People returned to live there. The young people, my generation—those of us who were raised mostly in exile or with resentment—returned too. From the late 1990s until at least 2006, Lebanon became a paradise regained for those of us who had lost it as children. It was a country that had reversed its course: people were no longer identified, judged, and separated by religion or sect. Instead the youth of Lebanon were united by their pride in being Lebanese. Although we each peppered our Arabic with English, French, German, or Spanish—although some wore crosses and some wore headscarves—we still managed to communicate and engage in life together. Somehow, despite Teta's fears, our resilient parents and grandparents had indeed managed to instill a love of this tiny, quirky, Mediterranean home in all of us.

And then, in July of 2006, the bombs began to fall again. I was alone in Lebanon that summer, and overnight, the country was transformed from a summer idyll into a chaotic, fearful, broken country. I retreated to the mountains with my family, where it was safer, and helped to distract my cousin's young daughters, whose parents had gone out of the country without their girls for the first time ever. Layla, four, and Iman, two, giggled and chatted and played; every once in a while they swallowed the spaghetti I fed them. While I was with them I remembered myself at the age of three or four in Beirut, eating *cousa* (stuffed courgettes) with my brother on Teta's balcony, blissfully unaware that a war raged not far from us. Watching the girls, I suddenly realized that I was now in the position my aunts, uncles, parents, and grandparents had been in when I was a child.

A wave of panic gripped me when I understood that I was the veteran here and that I was somehow responsible for future generations. So many of my peers felt the same. But despite our fear, we became incredibly motivated—we wrote; we blogged; we petitioned; we protested; we created art, music, and theatre; we plastered cities all over the world with stickers saying, "I love Beirut." We would not let Lebanon bleed to death again. There was no sense of resignation; there was a knowledge that the madness *would* end, and we *would* return. It occurs to me that this might have been perceived as some sort of intense nationalism, a pride of place and love of country, but as I think about it, what we were all doing, in fact, was displaying the exact sort of humanism that Teta embraced. I think she would have been proud.

Historical Overview

∾

MARIAM C. SAID

Wadad Makdisi Cortas was born in 1909, the end of the first decade of the twentieth century in Beirut. At that time present-day Lebanon, Syria, Palestine, and Jordan were under Ottoman rule (actually Beirut was an Ottoman province). When she was born, the coastal cities of Lebanon—namely, Tripoli, Beirut, and Sidon—were not part of the Mutassarrifiya, which was the autonomous province of Mount Lebanon that comprised Mount Lebanon and the coast between Beirut and Tripoli.

Soon after the outbreak of World War I the Mutassarrifiya was abolished. In 1916 famine hit Beirut and Mount Lebanon. Wadad Makdisi Cortas alludes to that, but her story begins with her first memories in 1917, one year later, when the effects of the famine were everywhere to be seen.

In 1920 at the San Remo conference, France was granted a mandate over Lebanon and Syria; Britain was given a mandate over Palestine and Iraq, and in Palestine despite the existence of a huge Arab majority, the British implemented a mandate explicitly committed to the creation of a Jewish national home. That year in July the French overthrew the Arab government of Faysal, son of the Sharif Husayn, in Damascus, and by the beginning of September, the French declared the establishment of Greater Lebanon. The coastal cities of Sidon, Beirut, and Tripoli became part of Greater Lebanon. Beirut was designated the capital of the new entity.

In 1926 the Lebanese Constitution was promulgated. Ten years later, in 1936, the French Lebanese Independence Treaty was signed.

In 1936 to 1939 a general strike and revolt occurred in Palestine against the British mandate because the Arabs of Palestine were opposed to the creation of a Jewish state in their country.

In 1943 a crisis erupted in November between the Lebanese and the French. The French mandate was terminated, and November 22, 1943, became the official date of independence for present-day Lebanon.

In May 1948 the war in Palestine took place, and in March 1949 a coup d'état overthrew the Syrian regime. Later that year the Lebanese signed an armistice with Israel.

In 1950 the Syrian and Lebanese Customs Union broke up.

In 1952 a coup d'état by the military overthrew the monarchy in Egypt. A year later Gamal Abdel Nasser became the president of Egypt.

In 1953 women were granted the right to vote in Lebanon, and they participated in the summer elections that year.

In 1953 a military coup in Iran overthrew the democratically elected government of Mohammad Mosaddeq and returned the Shah to power.

In 1955 the Baghdad Pact was signed between Turkey and Iraq.

In July 1956 Nasser nationalized the Suez Canal, and in October of that year the Suez War took place, which was an invasion of Egypt by Israel, Britain, and France.

In February 1958 the United Arab Republic (UAR), a union between Egypt and Syria, was declared. In May an armed revolt against the president of the Republic of Lebanon erupted that lasted for over three months. U.S. marines were sent to Lebanon and by the end of the summer a new president was inaugurated.

During the summer of 1958, on July 14, a revolution took place in Iraq.

In September 1961 the UAR broke up.

The 1961–1962 New Year's Eve failed coup d'état was attempted in Lebanon by the Syrian Nationalist Socialist Party (SNSP), a Lebanese secular party.

In March 1963 a military coup d'état by Baathists and Arab Nationalists took place in Syria.

In June 1967 the Arab Israeli War took place.

In 1970 Hafiz al Assad attained power in Syria. In September of that year the PLO clashed with the Jordanian government ("Black September") and was expelled from Jordan. Nasser of Egypt died.

In April 1975 civil war erupted in Lebanon. It would last for fifteen years.

In November 1977 Anwar Sadat, the president of Egypt, visited Israel.

In March 1978 the Israeli Army invaded southern Lebanon and established a proxy army to patrol a buffer zone they established on Lebanese territory.

In January 1979 the Islamic Revolution in Iran overthrew the Shah's regime.

Wadad Makdisi Cortas died in May of 1979.

In 1982 Israel invaded Lebanon. The horrors of Lebanon's civil war continued until 1990.

After the end of the civil war, a period of calm ensued. A massive reconstruction of downtown Beirut took place. Israeli invasions and occupation continued until 2000.

In 2005 the Lebanese prime minister, Rafic Harriri, was assassinated.

In the summer of 2006 the Lebanon Israel War erupted.

As of 2009, the situation in Lebanon remains unsettled.

Acknowledgments

On the 100th anniversary of my mother's birth, her wish to have her memoir published in English has been realized, thanks to all the friends and relatives who have contributed in this endeavor. The list of friends and relatives who read the manuscript over the past thirty years and their valuable advice is long, and they will forgive me for not mentioning each and every one of them by name, but I am most grateful for their encouragement and input. Nevertheless, I would like to thank in particular the support of Deirdre Bergson, the first person to read the manuscript; Dolly Stade, who was the first to work on editing the manuscript; and John Pickering, for his help early on. I would also like to thank Sandra Fahy, my husband Edward's assistant, for helping me in scanning the manuscript. Most of all I would like to acknowledge with gratitude Zia Jaffrey, one of the many readers of the manuscript, who had the insight in 2002 to nudge me and insist that I try and publish this work. She had recognized that the time had come for this story to be told. Without the help of both Zia and JoAnn Wypijewski, the final editor of the memoir, this book would not have materialized. The three of us worked as a team over a long period of time, and I am indebted to them and gratefully acknowledge them. Thanks also to the Wylie Agency, and in particular Jin Auh, Tracy Bohan, Sarah Chalfant, and Jacqueline Ko; and to Nation Books, especially my editor Ruth Baldwin and project editor Michelle Welsh-Horst, who made the process very smooth and were great to work with.

I am deeply saddened that Edward did not live to see this book come to fruition. Mother entrusted him with the manuscript a few weeks before she passed away. Over the years he helped me immensely, showering advice and offering excellent ideas. We spent many years thinking and talking about how to publish this book. He was still alive when I revived the project, and discussed it with JoAnn, Zia, and me. Without his help, support, and love, I would not have been able to realize Mother's wish. I felt he was always there guiding me along every step of the way. To Edward, I am most grateful.

Mariam C. Said

Notes

⌖

CHAPTER 1

1. At the time Beirut, along with most of the coastal region that is now part of Lebanon, was part of Syria. For centuries the name "Lebanon" had been associated only with the central mountain mass of Syria, including the Lebanon Mountains and the Anti-Lebanon Mountains, separated by the Bekaa Valley. Beginning in the late nineteenth century the term "Lebanon" was used primarily in reference to the western range of this mountain mass, bordered on the north by the Akkar region, on the west by the Mediterranean coast, on the south by the Litani River, and on the east by Bekaa. Sometimes called "Mount Lebanon" or "The Lebanon," this western range had a singularly complex population of about 400,000 in 1900, composed of Maronite, Eastern Orthodox, and Greek Uniate Christians; Sunni and Shiite Muslims; and Druze. A quarrelsome, politically volatile, nonreligious but highly class-conscious region, it was difficult to administer, and in the 1860s the Ottomans made it an autonomous region, extending westward to the coast, with the exception of the main cities, Tripoli, Beirut, and Sidon, which remained part of Syria, as did the Bekaa plain and the Anti-Lebanon Mountains. These areas are what the author in 1917 would have understood to be Lebanon (or Mount Lebanon) and Syria.

2. Set up by American missionaries in the nineteenth century, the institution was renamed on November 18, 1920, shortly after the establishment of Greater Lebanon by the French in August of that year.

CHAPTER 2

1. The Akkar region is part of present-day Lebanon. At the time of the narrative it was part of Syria.

CHAPTER 5

1. In the summer of 1924 the talk revolved around the popular revolution in Sudan, which was spearheaded by the White Banner Society under the slogan

"Unity of the Nile Valley" and demanded "to unite Egypt and Sudan under one crown, one parliament and one law" independent of British colonial rule. Unity of the Nile, however, had been a subject of keen interest in intellectual circles for years. The context for Dumit's observation here is unclear, since by that summer, with throngs of demonstrators in Khartoum invoking Saad Zaghlul and calling for the fall of Britain, the British were set on severing Sudan from Egypt once and for all. It had not always been thus. The Anglo-Egyptian condominium of 1899 established joint control over Sudan, a kind of unity in which Egypt was decidedly the junior partner and Sudan a de facto ward of Britain but which did recognize the territorial integrity of the Nile Valley and the shared history of its people. Following the Egyptian popular revolution of 1919 and Britain's unilateral declaration of Egyptian independence under King Fouad in 1922, the British were determined to confine nationalist passions, declaring the question of Sudan as one "absolutely reserved to the discretion" of the British government. Nationalists insisted otherwise, and from 1922 on *Al-Ahram* in Cairo and other newspapers promoted an energetic discussion over the unity of the Nile. By the end of 1924 colonial repression and manipulation of Sudanese religious figures and others had put an end to nationalist unity and Egyptian influence, and Britain began administering Sudan as essentially two colonies, north and south, the effects of which persist today.

CHAPTER 6

1. The declaration was conveyed in a letter to Lord Rothschild, head of the Zionist Federation in Great Britain. Balfour, then British foreign secretary, stated, "His Majesty's Government views with favour the establishment in Palestine of a national home for the Jewish people, and will use their best endeavours to facilitate the achievement of this object, it being clearly understood that nothing should be done which may prejudice the civil and religious rights of existing non-Jewish communities in Palestine, or the rights and political status enjoyed by Jews in any other country." Although the text, originally submitted in more certain terms by Rothschild in a letter to Balfour and then revised and approved by the British cabinet in its final form, makes no mention of a state, it was used by the Zionist Federation and other elements in the movement to create a Jewish state in Palestine. It was the first such formal expression of support by a world power for a Jewish "national home."

CHAPTER 14

1. Among attacks attributed to the Zionist terrorist organization Irgun in 1938 were the bombing of a train on April 12 and a cafe on April 17, both in Haifa; an attack on a bus in Jerusalem on May 17; a bombing in Jaffa on June 26; a bus bombing in Jerusalem on July 5; two bombings in a market in Haifa

on July 6; a bombing in Jerusalem on July 8; and marketplace bombings in Jerusalem, Haifa, and Jaffa on July 16, July 25, and August 26. Bombings of Arab marketplaces, a cinema, and other public places continued through 1939. All of these were in addition to actions by the Jewish Settlement Police and its offshoots, including the Special Night Squads, which were set up by the British and worked in tandem with British efforts to crush the revolt. Some historians estimate that from 1936 to 1939 more than 10 percent of Arab men in Palestine were detained, wounded, or killed.

CHAPTER 17

1. Zurayk, a major activist intellectual, was also a member of the family, having married Najla Cortas, Emile's sister and Wadad's sister-in-law. A professor of history at the American University in Beirut and Syria's delegate to the United Nations in 1946–47, Zurayk is renowned for his 1948 book *The Meaning of Disaster* (in Arabic, *Ma'na al-Nakba*) in which he coined the term "Nakba," or "catastrophe," widely used by Palestinians and others in the Arab world to refer to the 1948 Arab-Israeli war. He was also one of the founders, with Wadad Cortas and others, of the Institute for Palestine Studies in 1963 and its chairman until 1984.

CHAPTER 18

1. As the Pakistani activist intellectual Eqbal Ahmad put it succinctly, the Zionists secretly opposed the Partition Plan but made a tactical decision to accept it publicly. The Arabs openly opposed the plan and made the strategic blunder of openly rejecting it. By the beginning of 1949 the Zionists had forcibly annexed about 22 percent more of the land than was allocated to them by the Partition Plan.

2. A *New York Times* reporter gave a detailed account of these events on April 10, 1948. The *Times* reported 254 dead. Soon after, the leadership of the Haganah disavowed any participation and condemned the attack as the work of rogue terrorists. Many years later, in the 1980s, long after Wadad Cortas had died, Birzeit University as well as Israeli scholars conducted investigations affirming the Haganah role and determining that about 120 villagers had been massacred.

3. Lundstrom was the head of UN truce supervision in Palestine at the time and Bernadotte's personal representative. Subsequent scholars have determined that the murder was executed by Lehi (a.k.a. the Stern Gang) and approved by its central leadership, which included future Israeli Prime Minister Yitzhak Shamir. After the assassination Prime Minister David Ben-Gurion ordered Lehi to be disbanded and its members arrested. One of its leaders and one member were tried and convicted of membership in a terrorist organization, but Ben-Gurion pardoned them after they spent two weeks in jail. As Kati Marton noted in her book *A Death in Jerusalem*,

"Not one of the hit team would ever spend a night in jail or face a court of justice." The shooter, Yehoshua Cohen, later became Ben-Gurion's personal bodyguard. Natan Yellin-Mor, in the central leadership with Shamir, which dispatched the killers, was elected to the first Knesset. Lehi's Jerusalem operations chief, Yehoshua Zetler, acknowledged the group's responsibility for the murders in an interview with the Israeli press in 1977, the thirtieth anniversary of the atrocity and six years after the statute of limitations had expired.

CHAPTER 19

1. Sir John Bagot Glubb (Glubb Pasha), a British soldier first posted to Iraq under the Mandate in 1920, commanded the Arab Legion throughout World War II and then until 1956. During the 1948 war he complained that "internecine struggles . . . are more in the minds of Arab politicians than the struggle against the Jews."

CHAPTER 22

1. Also known, at different times, as the Central Treaty Organization (CENTO) and the Middle East Treaty Organization (METO), the Baghdad Pact was a regional alliance organized as part of the West's containment policy toward the Soviet Union. The United States joined the alliance in 1959.

2. This is not to say there was no opposition. From the beginning, the pro-king elements, supporters of the old regime, and pro-Western elements opposed Nasser, as did the Communist Party and the Muslim Brothers. The general population, however, did not. That attitude changed somewhat following the Suez Crisis and the more extensive nationalization policies of the late 1950s, when "foreigners"—many of whom had lived their whole lives in the country, regarded themselves as Egyptian, and originally supported Nasser—found they could no longer work and emigrated from Egypt. Even before the Suez Canal was nationalized, the situation of Jewish Egyptians was complicated by the Lavon Affair, in which the Israeli secret service planted bombs in Egypt to scare the Jewish population into emigrating. Many of them did, and some went to Israel. Internally, Nasser felt most threatened by the Communist Party and the Muslim Brothers, and he went after both. Many Communists were imprisoned, and some managed to leave the country. The Muslim Brothers had a worse fate, and after a group of them tried to assassinate Nasser in the late 1950s, he went after them with a vengeance.

CHAPTER 24

1. That year UNESCO held a conference on women's education in Algeria; Wadad Cortas attended as an observer on behalf of the International Women's Council.

CHAPTER 25

1. For some time Israel had launched raids and outright assaults on Jordanian territory, and Israeli settlers in the Golan region had, by former Israeli Defense Minister Moshe Dayan's admission, been used to provoke Syrian attacks. "We would send a tractor to plow some area where it wasn't possible to do anything, in the demilitarized area, and knew in advance that the Syrians would start to shoot. If they didn't shoot, we would tell the tractor to advance further, until in the end the Syrians would get annoyed and shoot. And then we would use artillery and later the air force also, and that's how it was," Dayan said in an interview with the *New York Times* in 1997. Border clashes with Syria escalated to dogfights and air assaults in the months before the June war, with some Israeli military and political figures threatening to attack Damascus, overthrow the government, and occupy Syria. In May, Soviet intelligence reports (faulty, as it turns out) that Israeli troops were massing along the Syrian border prompted Egypt, allied with Syria, to mobilize its forces in the Sinai.

2. In the event, Israel declared the closing of the straits an act of war by "strangulation" and used it to justify its surprise attack on Egypt, annihilating the Egyptian air force. Officially Israel has always called the 1967 war "pre-emptive," citing Egypt's mobilization and bombastic rhetoric as proof of imminent attack. The British and U.S. governments—which, along with the French, had armed Israel for years—were not so sure, and while they condemned Egypt's closing of the straits, they refused Israel's request to launch an immediate maritime expedition to force open the waterway. CIA and Pentagon assessments at the time held that Egyptian forces were in defensive positions, that Nasser had no intention of launching an offensive, and that in a match between Israeli and Arab forces, the former had "qualitative superiority" and were likely to prevail. Egypt's vice president had been scheduled to meet U.S. officials in Washington to discuss a diplomatic solution when Israel attacked on June 5. In 1982 Prime Minister Menachem Begin told the Israeli National Defense College that "the Egyptian army concentrations in the Sinai approaches do not prove that Nasser was about to attack us. We must be honest with ourselves. We decided to attack him."

3. At Karameh, Palestinian commandos were joined by Jordanian forces. The PLO had been established by the Arab League in 1964, at which time it consisted largely of Palestinian units integrated into the armies of Egypt, Syria, Jordan, and Iraq. By the fall of 1967, with the Arab states defeated and in disarray, it emerged as an autonomous organization (albeit heavily subsidized by the Arab states), a confederation of parties, divided between nationalists and Marxists. Fatah, a nationalist organization established by exiles in Egypt in the late 1950s and guided by the idea that Palestinians must have primary responsibility for the liberation of Palestine, spoke to the extreme distress of refugees, advocated guerrilla war, and was central in the battle of Karameh. It joined the PLO and, in the person of Yasir Arafat, dominated its leadership by 1969.

CHAPTER 26

1. Meanwhile, internal political calculations divided the Arabs. The rise of the PLO as a popular force in the refugee camps and among Arab youth was seen as a threat by state leaders, who, first in Syria and then in Jordan, brutally expelled the Palestinian fighters, massacring civilians and forcing the PLO to re-establish itself in southern Lebanon by 1971.

2. The Barlev Line was a series of earthen ramparts and concrete fortifications built by the Israelis along the eastern rim of the Suez Canal after they occupied the Sinai Peninsula following the 1967 war.

3. Said was also Wadad Cortas's son-in-law by this time.

CHAPTER 27

1. The Lebanese government, under the control of elite conservative Christian parties, was being increasingly pressured by the progressive, secular, and left parties that coalesced in the Lebanese National Movement. The LNM represented Druze, Sunnis, some Shiites, some Christians allied with the PLO, a number of socialist parties, and the Communist Party. Central to its program were secularism, Arabism, and support for the Palestinians, as well as an end to the Christian parties' monopoly on governance. For most of the civil war the PLO allied with the LNM. Arrayed on the other side was the Christian Lebanese Front, which included the right-wing Phalange and other Christian factions, some Shiites, and parts of the government. The Lebanese Front opposed the PLO presence in southern Lebanon and in the camps in Beirut. During the war it would receive arms, advisers, and tanks from Israel.

CHAPTER 28

1. At different times in the lead-up to war and during the years of fighting, Syria or pro-Syrian factions allied with the LNM and the PLO, with the right-wing Lebanese Front, and with the remnant of the Lebanese government. By June 1976 President Suleiman Frangieh, Sarkis's predecessor, formally called on Syria to intervene, and Syrian troops occupied Tripoli and the Bekaa Valley. Forces sympathetic to Frangieh were by then also receiving military aid from Israel. By October, when the Arab League's Riyadh Accord provided for an Arab Deterrent Force to separate Lebanon's warring factions, Syria was supplying most of the troops to that force and soon occupied much of the country officially as a peacekeeper.